Manna For The Spirit

Dear Joyce,

May this book bring you

Peace, Love, Joy and the
Knowledge that God loves you
and so do I.

— Jay

Written By

Dr. Jay Korsen

This book is dedicated to my wife Lori, the mother of my two beautiful children Ryan and Lindsay. I am honored and privileged to be married to a woman of deep faith who loves Jesus and is a true prayer warrior.

A special thank you to Wheeler Van Brocklin and Paul Buterbaugh whom I have met every Thursday morning for the last 15 years or so to study the Bible and support each other in our walk with Jesus Christ our Lord and Savior.

Introduction

I began writing a daily reflection on Facebook several years ago after being inspired by daily messages I used to receive on my cell phone from what is now known as Gotandem.com. The messages seemed to speak directly to me and answered many of my biblical questions. I shared the messages with friends online and soon began receiving biblical questions from those friends who mistakenly thought I wrote the daily reflections. In an attempt to answer their questions, I used a similar format as Gotandem.com, did my research and posted the answers.

Over time, I began studying the Bible each morning or night for an hour or two to answer my own difficult questions with biblically sound answers. At the end of my daily study, I would try to summarize the answers I found in what my friends began calling my "Bible minute". I try to pick tough, modern day, real life questions to answer biblically but this is truly just an average guy's approach to trying to get to the truth.

You should know that I am a chiropractor in Narragansett, RI. I have been practicing chiropractic for 26 years so you'll see several references to my profession although it is not my intention to teach you anything about chiropractic in this devotional. I did write this devotional during a year that was plagued by one of the nastiest presidential elections in history so there will be several references to politics although it is not my intention to teach you anything about politics in this devotional.

I did go to Trinity College of the Bible for a year but I did my studies online and that was 15 years ago. You should know I didn't continue past my first year because I didn't think I was the guy to explain death or dying, especially if a child was involved, to a family. I didn't get it back then. Truthfully I still don't completely understand God's plan but I have found most of the answers in the Bible. Just like you, I don't like all the answers I've found, but I believe that God has a plan and I trust that plan. I now emphatically believe with all my heart that ALL THINGS work together for good as described in Romans 8:28.

On most of the pages that follow, I have left some space at the bottom for you to jot a few notes of your own about the reflection and verses each day. Don't feel you have to write only about what you read on the page. Dig deep and come up with your own tough questions and find the biblical answers on your own and then share them on this book's Facebook group called, "Manna For The Spirit". I would love to hear from you in that group and get your feedback on this devotional.

If you picked up this book and become inspired to learn more about biblical questions and answers, I'm going to advise you to join a Bible study. I'm a guy so the Men's Bible Study I formed at my old church turned out to be "just what the doctor ordered". At the time, I had a very enthusiastic pastor that helped me form the group. If you're a gal or a couple or a teen, form a group that you can relate to and pick a book or a study that's appropriate for your group. Ask at your church and get one started if there's not one available now.

Along the way, while reading this devotional, if you have a great Bible question that's tougher than you anticipated, don't despair. That happens to me all the time. Email me at drjaykorsen@aol.com and maybe I'll be able to help you out.

Enjoy the read. It's my prayer that the words that follow, from the Word, will inspire you, will increase your faith, will call you to action, and will warm your heart.

In Health and Faith,

Jay Korsen, DC

Day 1

Matthew 7:1-5
"Judge not, that you be not judged. For with the judgment
you pronounce you will be judged, and with the measure
you use it will be measured to you. Why do you see the
speck that is in your brother's eye, but do not notice the log
that is in your own eye? Or how can you say to your
brother, 'Let me take the speck out of your eye,' when there
is the log in your own eye? You hypocrite, first take the log
out of your own eye, and then you will see clearly to
take the speck out of your brother's eye.

There once was an old man with his young grandson and a
small donkey. The old man put the young boy on the small
donkey and began walking into town. Before long people
noticed the young boy on the small donkey and said aloud,
"Look at that young boy making that old man walk while
he rides. That's disrespectful!" Hearing that, the old man
took the young boy off the donkey and got on himself to
ride into town. Soon more onlookers began to say, "Look at
that grown man making that poor young boy walk beside
the donkey while he rides into town. What a shame!"
Responding to that, the old man reached down from the
donkey and picked the young boy up and put him on the
donkey beside him. Once again the onlookers sneered at
them and remarked, "I can not believe that old man and
young boy are both riding on that small donkey making it
do that back-breaking work! That is a sin!" Hearing that,
the old man and the young boy got off and carried the
donkey the rest of the way into town.

Proverbs 13:20
Whoever walks with the wise becomes wise, but the
companion of fools will suffer harm.
Proverbs 26:4
Don't answer the foolish arguments of fools, or you will
become as foolish as they are.
Acts 5:29
But Peter and the apostles answered, "We must obey God
rather than men.

Day 2

Does Jesus speak to people today either by talking aloud to them or by making a mental impression on them? Personally, I have never heard a voice claiming to be Jesus. I will admit that I've had an impression in the pit of my stomach that I felt was leading me in one direction or another or was an answer to prayer that I attributed to God through the Holy Spirit...

1 Corinthians 2:10
But God has shown us these things through the Spirit.
The Spirit knows all things. The Spirit even knows the deep secrets of God.
Ephesians 3:3-5
God himself showed me this secret plan of his, that the Gentiles, too, are included in his kindness. I say this to explain to you how I know about these things. In olden times God did not share this plan with his people, but now he has revealed it by the Holy Spirit to his apostles and prophets.
2 Timothy 3:16-17
The whole Bible was given to us by inspiration from God and is useful to teach us what is true and to make us realize what is wrong in our lives; it straightens us out and helps us do what is right. It is God's way of making us well prepared at every point, fully equipped to do good to everyone.
Proverbs 14:12
Before every man there lies a wide and pleasant road that seems right but ends in death.

There is no indication that Jesus or God speaks to anyone audibly today so don't feel as though you are being left out! Whether or not He is speaking to us through mental impressions is a tougher one to answer. Proverbs 14:12 speaks to the fact that we have to be careful to discern whether or not the "answers" we are getting by a "feeling" we get or an impression are from God or from our heart which can be deceitful. If we really want to hear Him speak to us today, we must listen to Him through His Word, The Holy Bible. (John 17:28)

Day 3

Baptism, or as my daughter used to say when she was little, "Bap-a-tism" can be a little confusing. So what is the importance of a Christian Baptism? There are so many questions people ask about this seemingly simple ordinance that Jesus instituted for the church. Some denominations feel that if it's not by submersion, it's not a "real" baptism. Some say if it's done before one is old enough to understand it's meaning, it doesn't count. Some say if it's not done just after birth, the child is not eligible to enter heaven if the unthinkable happens. So much confusion over a Gift, given to us by God! So what does the Bible say about Bap-a-tism?

Matthew 28:19–20
Go therefore and make disciples of all nations, baptizing them in the name of the Father and of the Son and of the Holy Spirit, teaching them to observe all that I have commanded you. And behold, I am with you always, to the end of the age."
Romans 6:4
We were buried therefore with him by baptism into death, in order that, just as Christ was raised from the dead by the glory of the Father, we too might walk in newness of life.
Acts 2:41
So those who received his word were baptized, and there were added that day about three thousand souls.
John 3:5
Jesus answered, "Truly, truly, I say to you, unless one is born of water and the Spirit, he cannot enter the kingdom of God

As we read above, baptism is actually a command from Jesus. The water cleanses us and prepares the way for Him to enter our hearts. Baptism represents the death, burial and resurrection of Jesus as well as our death to sin and the beginning of our new life with Christ. Biblically, baptism is a rite of identification with Christ, not a requirement for salvation or the entrance into heaven. If baptism were necessary it would be "works" and we cannot add our works to His grace. Never the less, Bap-a-tism is a beautiful outward expression of our love for God the Father, Jesus the Son and The Holy Spirit.

Day 4

There are some people that deny the existence of a place called Hell (or Sheol in Hebrew). I even had a pastor that argued that there was no such place and everyone wound up in heaven. It's the everyone get's a trophy mentality today that re-interprets biblical verses to say no matter what you believe or how much you sin, you wind up in heaven. Along the same lines, people deny the existence of the one that goes by the name of Satan, Devil, Deceiver, Lucifer, Prince of darkness and the enemy.

Isaiah 14:12-15
"How you are fallen from heaven, O Day Star, son of Dawn! How you are cut down to the ground, you who laid the nations low! You said in your heart, 'I will ascend to heaven; above the stars of God I will set my throne on high; I will sit on the mount of assembly in the far reaches of the north; I will ascend above the heights of the clouds; I will make myself like the Most High.' But you are brought down to Sheol, to the far reaches of the pit.
Revelation 12:7-9
Now war arose in heaven, Michael and his angels fighting against the dragon. And the dragon and his angels fought back, but he was defeated, and there was no longer any place for them in heaven. And the great dragon was thrown down, that ancient serpent, who is called the devil and Satan, the deceiver of the whole world—he was thrown down to the earth, and his angels were thrown down with him.
2 Corinthians 11:14

And no wonder, for even Satan disguises himself as an angel of light. Perhaps the fact that the Bible mentions Lucifer by name and that his first home was indeed heaven, is proof enough that he's not just a fictional character or some guy dressed up in a red Halloween costume. Denial (D-Nile) is a place in Egypt. Know your enemy. "If you know the enemy and know yourself, you need not fear the result of a hundred battles. If you know yourself but not the enemy, for every victory gained you will also suffer a defeat. If you know neither the enemy nor yourself, you will succumb in every battle." –Sun Tzu

Day 5

Have you ever noticed that in John 8:16 when a "band" came with Judas to arrest Jesus, He asked whom they were looking for? They replied that they were looking for Jesus of Nazareth. Jesus told them, I Am He. When He said this, the "band" of between 180 and 500 soldiers all "went backwards and fell to the ground". 180- 500 soldiers were helpless and unable to go forward and bind Jesus to take Him away.

John 18:1-9

When Jesus had spoken these words, he went forth with his disciples over the brook Cedron, where was a garden, into the which he entered, and his disciples.

2 And Judas also, which betrayed him, knew the place: for Jesus ofttimes resorted thither with his disciples.

3 Judas then, having received a band of men and officers from the chief priests and Pharisees, cometh thither with lanterns and torches and weapons.

4 Jesus therefore, knowing all things that should come upon him, went forth, and said unto them, Whom seek ye?

5 They answered him, Jesus of Nazareth. Jesus saith unto them, I am he. And Judas also, which betrayed him, stood with them.

6 As soon then as he had said unto them, I am he, they went backward, and fell to the ground.

7 Then asked he them again, Whom seek ye? And they said, Jesus of Nazareth.

8 Jesus answered, I have told you that I am he: if therefore ye seek me, let these go their way:

9 That the saying might be fulfilled, which he spake, Of them which thou gavest me have I lost none.

So many important things going on here! First, they felt they needed literally hundreds of men to arrest Jesus. Jesus reveals who He is with the phrase I AM HE. I AM is, of course, the name God reveals Himself as to Moses. Thus, Jesus reveals Himself as God. To this, the soldiers find themselves powerless, fall backwards and onto the ground, not with force but due to the Power in the Name. Also, notice in verse 8, He surrenders Himself so that his trembling disciples may go free which is a foreshadowing of the sacrifice He makes willingly for Us. God stood between his disciples and evil just as He stands between us and evil today. They had no power to arrest him, HE CHOSE TO SURRENDER FOR YOU. He died because He chose, He chose because He loved. Similarly, we have free will. God chose not to have the power to make us love or accept Him. It is our choice. WILL YOU CHOSE TO SURRENDER TO HIM?

Day 6

There was an old song when I was a kid called Looking for Love. The verse went something like this: "I was lookin' for love in all the wrong places, Lookin' for love in too many faces…I was alone then, no love in sight, I did everything I could to get me through the night." There's one love that's looking for you right now. There's one love that will fill your heart with joy and contentment. That love is God's love for you. Here is what that love looks like.

1 John 4:8
Anyone who does not love does not know God, because God is love.
Romans 8:37-39
No, in all these things we are more than conquerors through him who loved us. For I am sure that neither death nor life, nor angels nor rulers, nor things present nor things to come, nor powers, nor height nor depth, nor anything else in all creation, will be able to separate us from the love of God in Christ Jesus our Lord.
John 3:16
"For God so loved the world, that he gave his only Son, that whoever believes in him should not perish but have eternal life.
John 15:12
"This is my commandment, that you love one another as I have loved you.

God already loves you just the way you are. If you are ready to accept His love, just repeat this simple prayer: Lord Jesus, I repent of my sins. Come into my heart and I will make you my lord and savior. AMEN. If you sincerely prayed that prayer, I believe you have been born again of the Spirit. The next step is to find a church in your area to learn more about God's love. By the way, the song ends with the lyrics, "God bless the day I discovered you, oh you, lookin' for love." God bless you and this day indeed.

Day 7

I was told by a friend today that they feel "stuck in their life. They had been "dealt a bad hand" and they were having a hard time focusing on anything but the negatives in their life. They were even beginning to have negative self talk anticipating more bad things that were going to happen to them. Ever felt that way yourself? Maybe your finances spiraled out of control or your marriage hit rock bottom or Maybe you lost your job or decided to leave your church. Maybe a close friendship is failing and needs repairing. Here is some advice from the Word...

Isaiah 43:1-2, 4-5
Israel, the Lord who created you says, "Do not be afraid—I will save you. I have called you by name—you are mine. When you pass through deep waters, I will be with you; your troubles will not overwhelm you. When you pass through fire, you will not be burned; the hard trials that come will not hurt you... I will give up whole nations to save your life, because you are precious to me and because I love you and give you honor. Do not be afraid—I am with you!
Psalm 119: 37
Keep me from paying attention to what is worthless; be good to me, as you have promised.
Isaiah 43:18
But the Lord says, "Do not cling to events of the past or dwell on what happened long ago.
Philippians 4:12-13
I know what it is to be in need, and I know what it is to have plenty. I have learned the secret of being content in any and every situation, whether well fed or hungry, whether living in plenty or in want. I can do all this through Him who gives me strength.

When we focus on ourselves and our current situation, things can look dire. But, if we change our focus to what God's will for us is, the world becomes a brighter place. Instead of lamenting on what happened in the past, a bright new future filled with possibilities appears. The moment we realize how small our problems are and how Awesome and Big our God is becomes the moment we are "un-stuck", the scales fall off our eyes, and we begin to see things as they truly are for the very first time.

Day 8

Most of us know the story of Job in the Bible. He was a servant of God. Job was described by God as blameless and upright, God fearing and always turned from evil. Yet, still, God allowed Job to be tested by Satan. Job lost literally ALL he had and suffered greatly yet he never turned away or cursed God for his circumstances. In the end, God restored all Job had with twice as much as he had before.

Job 1:1
There was a man in the land of Uz whose name was Job, and that man was blameless and upright, one who feared God and turned away from evil.
Job 1:20-22 (After he was told all his livestock and his children were dead)
Then Job arose and tore his robe and shaved his head and fell on the ground and worshiped. And he said, "Naked I came from my mother's womb, and naked shall I return. The Lord gave, and the Lord has taken away; blessed be the name of the Lord." In all this Job did not sin or charge God with wrong.
Romans 8:28
And we know that all things work together for good to them that love God, to them who are the called according to his purpose.
1 Thessalonians 5:16-18
Rejoice evermore. Pray without ceasing. In every thing give thanks: for this is the will of God in Christ Jesus concerning you.

When confronted with horrific events in our lives, like Job was, we have 3 choices: 1) Complain, become bitter, curse God and lose faith. 2) Remain silent in faith while grieving. 3) REJOICE knowing that God has worked ALL THINGS out for good in the end. If you can find no reason to give thanks and your grief precludes your ability to rejoice, just PRAY knowing that your Father in heaven is listening and knows exactly how you feel. Through prayer, with time, to your own amazement, you will find yourself able to experience joy through the PEACE from the Lord that surpasses all understanding and you will once again be able to give thanks.

Day 9

The Bible warns that there will always be wars and rumors of wars. Nationally and globally there will be discord and a lack of peace and harmony. Sometimes it seems worse than other times and we feel disempowered and unable to do anything about it. The Bible gives good advice on making a difference in this world...

Matthew 28:18-20
And Jesus came and said to them, "All authority in heaven and on earth has been given to me. Go therefore and make disciples of all nations, baptizing them in the name of the Father and of the Son and of the Holy Spirit, teaching them to observe all that I have commanded you. And behold, I am with you always, to the end of the age."
Matthew 25:31-40
"When the Son of Man comes in his glory, and all the angels with him, then he will sit on his glorious throne. Before him will be gathered all the nations, and he will separate people one from another as a shepherd separates the sheep from the goats. And he will place the sheep on his right, but the goats on the left. Then the King will say to those on his right, 'Come, you who are blessed by my Father, inherit the kingdom prepared for you from the foundation of the world. For I was hungry and you gave me food, I was thirsty and you gave me drink, I was a stranger and you welcomed me, I was naked and you clothed me, I was sick and you visited me, I was in prison and you came to me.'

Jesus gave some really good advice that can be summarized by the phrase, "Think globally, act locally." To all those you encounter, share the Good News for starters. Then, feed the hungry in your community, give water to the thirsty, welcome strangers, donate clothes to people who do not have the means to buy them, comfort the sick and shut-ins, and visit or write letters of encouragement to people in prison. Individually, we may not be able to bring down the national debt but we can love our neighbor. Be a sheep, not a goat.

Day 10

In life, competitions will produce winners and losers. Contrary to popular belief today, not everyone deserves a trophy "just for competing". The side effect of having winners and losers is the fact that someone is going to win and unfortunately, like it or not, someone is going to lose. Perhaps the most valuable lesson we can learn in life from competing is how to become a "good sport" whether we win or lose.

Philippians 2:3
Do nothing from rivalry or conceit, but in humility count others more significant than yourselves.
Proverbs 24:17-18
Do not rejoice when your enemy falls, and let not your heart be glad when he stumbles, lest the Lord see it and be displeased, and turn away his anger from him.
1 Corinthians 9:24
Do you not know that in a race all the runners run, but only one receives the prize? So run that you may obtain it.
Philippians 3:14
I press on toward the goal for the prize of the upward call of God in Christ Jesus.

If you win, do it with humility. If you lose, be the first to congratulate the winner. We can learn more about ourselves and our character when we come in 4th place then when we go home clutching onto gold, silver or bronze medals. Whether we win or lose during this life means little compared to the prize that is to come when the race is over here on Earth and we enter into the presence of God and dwell forever in His Shekinah glory.

Day 11

Well, many of us have something in common on our minds the day before an election…decision making. Can we call on God to help us make a decision about who to vote for? In the grand scheme of things, voting is not that important compared to the kingdom of heaven. Even so, how can the Bible help us make important decisions in our lives?

1 Kings 3:9
So give Your servant an understanding heart to judge Your people to discern between good and evil. For who is able to judge this great people of Yours?"
Isaiah 30:21
And your ears shall hear a word behind you, saying, "This is the way, walk in it," when you turn to the right or when you turn to the left.
Proverbs 3:6
In all your ways acknowledge him, and he will make straight your paths.
1 John 5:14
And this is the confidence that we have toward him, that if we ask anything according to his will he hears us.
Proverbs 11:14
Where there is no guidance, a people falls, but in an abundance of counselors there is safety.

Pray for discernment; listen to that wee voice within, that feeling deep within your stomach; trust that the voice is indeed God; be confident that God will answer our questions according to His will; AND listen to the people he has placed in your life to guide and counsel you. Now that's not that tough…Is It?

Day 12

We've all been given a few "thorns in the side" in our lifetime. So, what's the deal? They are a gift from God. Paul, the author of most of the New Testament had a thorn in his side. Paul speaks of a "thorn in the flesh". He calls it "a messenger of Satan" that had a purpose of "torment." Paul talks about this "thorn in his side" metaphorically as a source of great pain in his life. Paul goes on to explain the purpose of this thorn…

2 Corinthians 12:7
So to keep me from becoming conceited because of the surpassing greatness of the revelations, a thorn was given me in the flesh, a messenger of Satan to harass me, to keep me from becoming conceited.
2 Corinthians 12:8-10
Concerning this I implored the Lord three times that it might leave me. And He has said to me, "My grace is sufficient for you, for power is perfected in weakness." Most gladly, therefore, I will rather boast about my weaknesses, so that the power of Christ may dwell in me. Therefore I am well content with weaknesses, with insults, with distresses, with persecutions, with difficulties, for Christ's sake; for when I am weak, then I am strong.

So, God's goal in allowing the thorn in the flesh was to keep Paul HUMBLE. Listen, no one likes to have aggravations or distractions in their lives but if you haven't had one yet, you soon will. Everyone experiences it at one point or another. Even Paul sought God to remove his "thorn" three times…to no avail. God has put a "thorn (or several thorns) in your flesh" to make sure your PRIDE does not get in your way of fulfilling His plan for you here on Earth. Just like Paul, instead of having the pain of your thorn removed, you'll receive overwhelming GRACE and STRENGTH instead to compensate for it.

Day 13

Anxiety and depression are so prevalent today. Everywhere we turn, stress is on the rise. Our food supply is tainted with genetically modified organisms (GMO's) and hosts of chemicals that make it unrecognizable as a "food" putting chemical stress on us. You only have to turn the TV on or read the news online to get your fill of mental stress. Technology has caused us to hang our heads down and stay seated for long periods of time putting more physical stress on us. Antidepressants are being used by nearly 40% of the population. What are we to do to combat the anxiety and depression? Well, the Bible has a few suggestions…

Isaiah 41:10
Fear not, for I am with you; be not dismayed, for I am your God; I will strengthen you, I will help you, I will uphold you with my righteous right hand.
Philippians 4:6-8
Do not be anxious about anything, but in everything by prayer and supplication with thanksgiving let your requests be made known to God. And the peace of God, which surpasses all understanding, will guard your hearts and your minds in Christ Jesus. Finally, brothers, whatever is true, whatever is honorable, whatever is just, whatever is pure, whatever is lovely, whatever is commendable, if there is any excellence, if there is anything worthy of praise, think about these things.
1 Peter 5:7
Casting all your anxieties on him, because he cares for you.
Proverbs 12:25
Anxiety in a man's heart weighs him down, but a good word makes him glad.
Matthew 6:34
"Therefore do not be anxious about tomorrow, for tomorrow will be anxious for itself. Sufficient for the day is its own trouble.

OK, taking advice is sometimes easier said than done. How about a practical piece of advice? Stress causes the muscles next to your spine to tighten and misalign. Those misalignments pinch nerves and interfere with the body's ability to heal itself like God designed it to do. Chiropractors locate and correct this interference called subluxations. Read your Bible daily to stay connected to God and let an ethical, principled, affordable chiropractor check your spine weekly for subluxations and correct them when found. How's that for a start?

Day 14

The Old Testament can often be difficult to read and even more often, difficult to interpret. One part that scholars and every day Bible readers like you and I have had a hard time with is figuring out what's going on with Ezekiel's Temple Vision. There is a temple with a Prince, sacrificial offerings, God departing and returning to the temple and lots and lots of details, some of which don't make sense after you read the New Testament… or maybe it does…

Ezekiel 43:4-5
And the glory and brilliance of the Lord entered the temple by way of the gate facing toward the east. Then the Spirit lifted me up and brought me into the inner courtyard; and behold, the glory and brilliance of the Lord filled the temple.
Ezekiel 43:10-11
"Son of man, describe the temple to the house of Israel, that they may be ashamed of their iniquities; and let them measure the pattern. And if they are ashamed of all that they have done, make known to them the design of the temple" (Ezek. 43:10–11).
Ezekiel 43:18
And He [the Lord] said to me, "Son of man, thus says the Lord God, 'These are the statutes and regulations for [the use of] the altar on the day that it is built, to offer burnt offerings on it and to sprinkle blood on it.

After reading Ezekiel for yourself, you may feel that the temple is the millennial temple for Jesus after his second coming. If that's true, then the sacrifices don't make sense because Jesus was the last and perfect sacrifice for sin. Maybe the sacrifices are just to commemorate Jesus' ultimate sacrifice. One thing is for sure, God describes this temple with dizzying detail so it's got to be important. Perhaps God gave us the plans because He knew one day the temple had to be built. Today let's reflect on the fact that God also gave us the entirety of the Bible to be used as a "plan" to show us how to "build" a life that is worthwhile and pleasing to Him. After all, we are the temple of the holy spirit 1 Corinthians 6:19.

Day 15

Have you ever sat by and watched two people disagree about something they both feel passionate about? As each person feels they are not being heard by the other, the volume of the voices gets higher and higher and the shouting match gets uglier and uglier. What does the Bible say about this kind of behavior?

Colossians 3:8
But now you must put them all away: anger, wrath, malice, slander, and obscene talk from your mouth.
Ephesians 4:29
Let no corrupting talk come out of your mouths, but only such as is good for building up, as fits the occasion, that it may give grace to those who hear.
Matthew 15:10-11
And he called the people to him and said to them, "Hear and understand: it is not what goes into the mouth that defiles a person, but what comes out of the mouth; this defiles a person."
Matthew 12:36-37
I tell you, on the day of judgment people will give account for every careless word they speak, for by your words you will be justified, and by your words you will be condemned."
James 3:10
From the same mouth come blessing and cursing. My brothers, these things ought not to be so.

Tact is the art of raising the eyebrows without raising the roof! Stephen Covey, in a book called The 7 Habits of Highly Successful People offers this advice: Seek first to understand, then, and only then, to be understood. As Christians, we are admonished to first be good listeners. Then, after we have listened respectfully, others will be more receptive when we share our Good News.

Day 16

We, as Americans, seem to have a "more is better" attitude. It's something that has been part of our culture for decades. As far back as the beginning of the 1900's, the famous singer/actor/public figure Mae West was quoted as saying, "If a little is great, and a lot is better, then way too much is just about right!" OR IS IT?

Exodus 16:4
"Then the LORD said to Moses, "I will rain down bread from heaven for you. The people are to go out each day and gather enough for that day. In this way I will test them and see whether they will follow my instructions."
Proverbs 25:16
If you have found honey, eat only enough for you, lest you have your fill of it and vomit it.
Proverbs 23:21
For the drunkard and the glutton will come to poverty, and slumber will clothe them with rags.
1 Timothy 6:10
For the love of money is a root of all kinds of evils. It is through this craving that some have wandered away from the faith and pierced themselves with many pangs.

All we really need is enough manna for today even though God will rain down abundance on us. The true test of a Christian is not whether or not he or she can build wealth. The true test is whether or not he or she uses the excess wealth to feed and clothe the poor and needy or whether he or she uses the excess all for themselves until they become physically sick and spiritually bankrupt. Sorry Mae West…A little honey is great, a lot of honey doesn't make it sweeter, and way too much will just make you sick. – That's Biblical!

Day 17

So, I've got some Good News and some bad news. The Good News is that God loves you. The bad news is that celebrating Halloween may not be in our best interests…

29 When he (God) destroys the nations in the land where you will live, 30 don't follow their example in worshiping their gods. Do not ask, 'How do these nations worship their gods?' and then go and worship as they do! 31 You must not insult the Lord your God like that! These nations have done HORRIBLE things that he hates, all in the name of their religion (Deuteronomy 12:29 - 31, see also Deuteronomy 18:11 - 12)
15 Do not love the world nor the things in the world. If anyone loves the world, the love of the Father is not in him (1John 2:15, NASB)

I'm not going to belabor this point as I myself have participated in what was started as the Celtic day of the dead since I was a small child. Though, to us, not God, it seems to be a harmless holiday, it most certainly is not a biblical holiday. When you think about it, really, it is just another chink in our spiritual armor. It is another example of how fortunate we are that there is grace where there should be judgment.

Write a few examples of when you received grace when you should have received judgment in your life:

Day 18

Humility is a VERY powerful thing. It's not easy, it's jut powerful. Our ego desires to be exalted among men and women. God asks us to be humble. Not an easy thing to do.

1 Peter 5:6
Humble yourselves, therefore, under the mighty hand of God so that at the proper time he may exalt you,
Matthew 23:12
Whoever exalts himself will be humbled, and whoever humbles himself will be exalted.
Micah 6:8
He has told you, O man, what is good; and what does the Lord require of you but to do justice, and to love kindness, and to walk humbly with your God?
Proverbs 3:34
Toward the scorners he is scornful, but to the humble he gives favor.

There will be times when we are honored for one of our achievements or we are recognized for one of our accomplishments. The ego wants to take the credit but God is admonishing to do something radical. He wants us to humble ourselves before Him. Lord God grant us the humility to accept the honors and recognition with grace and the wisdom to remain humble throughout the entire process.

Day 19

Exodus is defined as a journey by a group to escape from a hostile environment. Although it pertains to a group, we have all been in situations where we have been in a hostile environment and had to make our own personal exodus. There have been times when we thought there was no means of egress but somehow, God provided one...

Exodus 18:23
If you do this, God will direct you, you will be able to endure, and all this people also will go to their place in peace."
Jonah 1:17
And the Lord appointed a great fish to swallow up Jonah. And Jonah was in the belly of the fish three days and three nights.
Proverbs 22:3
The prudent sees danger and hides himself, but the simple go on and suffer for it.
Philippians 4:19
And my God will supply every need of yours according to his riches in glory in Christ Jesus.

It's not likely that God is going to send a big fish to rescue you in this day in age, but hey, who knows. All things are possible through Christ who strengthens us. When we are in a hostile environment, God will supply every need of ours. When we need to make an exodus from a hostile environment, just look for the WAY out... it's the TRUTH.

Day 20

Incorruptible. Now that's a cool concept! It means not being susceptible to corruption or bribery and not subject to death or decay, Everlasting. WOW…

Acts 26:23
that the Christ (the Messiah, the Anointed) was to suffer, and that He by being the first to rise from the dead [with an incorruptible body] would proclaim light (salvation) both to the Jewish people and to the Gentiles."
1 Corinthians 15:20
[The Order of Resurrection] But now [as things really are] Christ has in fact been raised from the dead, [and He became] the first fruits [that is, the first to be resurrected with an incorruptible, immortal body, foreshadowing the resurrection] of those who have fallen asleep [in death].
Ephesians 6:24
Grace be with all who love our Lord Jesus Christ with undying and incorruptible love.
Revelation 21:5
And He who sits on the throne said, "Behold, I am making all things new." Also He said, "Write, for these words are faithful and true [they are accurate, incorruptible, and trustworthy]."

No doubt, we are Corruptible due to temptation and free will which our fleshy body and material desires are wired to succumb to. With Christ we are made stronger and we are able to overcome many temptations. But, IN CHRIST we are made incorruptible! IN CHRIST, we are not subject to death or decay. IN CHRIST we are everlasting.

Day 21

Let's look at a word that is a little confusing at first, Sanctification. Things are sanctified when they are used for the purpose God intends. A human being is sanctified, therefore, when he or she lives according to God's design and purpose.

2 Timothy 2:21
Therefore, if anyone cleanses himself from what is dishonorable, he will be a vessel for honorable use, set apart as holy, useful to the master of the house, ready for every good work.
1 Thessalonians 5:23
Now may the God of peace himself sanctify you completely, and may your whole spirit and soul and body be kept blameless at the coming of our Lord Jesus Christ.
John 17:17
Sanctify them in the truth; your word is truth.
Galatians 2:20
I have been crucified with Christ. It is no longer I who live, but Christ who lives in me. And the life I now live in the flesh I live by faith in the Son of God, who loved me and gave himself for me.

Simply put, Sanctification is Sweet Surrender. The real sweetness of this surrender is the realization that God is willing to take all your hurt, pain and suffering and He replaces them with healing. Jesus came to set us free and show us the Way. The Way, of course, is our path to sanctification.

Day 22

Have you ever thought about how Rest and Restoration are tied into the Sabbath? Observing one day a week to take time to pause, worship God with other believers and be made whole again is part of His plan for our lives.

Exodus 20:8-11
"Remember the Sabbath day, to keep it holy. Six days you shall labor, and do all your work, but the seventh day is a Sabbath to the Lord your God. On it you shall not do any work, you, or your son, or your daughter, your male servant, or your female servant, or your livestock, or the sojourner who is within your gates. For in six days the Lord made heaven and earth, the sea, and all that is in them, and rested on the seventh day. Therefore the Lord blessed the Sabbath day and made it holy.
Psalm 23:2-3
He makes me lie down in green pastures. He leads me beside still waters. He restores my soul.
Zechariah 9:12
Return to your stronghold, O prisoners of hope; today I declare that I will restore to you double.

If you ask anyone the question, "When does the body heal itself?" The answer is obvious… when it's resting. On the Sabbath day God commands us to rest. In that rest, it is not just our physical body that is healed and restored to health, our soul is healed and we are made whole again. Before communion when we say, "Lord, I am not worthy that you should enter under my roof, but only say the Word and my soul shall be healed", we are asking God to come rest with us and restore us at our very core.

Day 23

Today let's focus on Gratitude. Recently a good friend had a serious challenge with his health. I'm sure we have all had to deal with this at one time or another. It's surreal when you spend time with someone one day and all seems fine and just a few short days later you get some unexpected news about them.

1 Thessalonians 5:18
Give thanks in all circumstances; for this is the will of God in Christ Jesus for you.
Hebrews 12:28
Therefore let us be grateful for receiving a kingdom that cannot be shaken, and thus let us offer to God acceptable worship, with reverence and awe,
Psalm 100:3-4
Know that the Lord, he is God! It is he who made us, and we are his; we are his people, and the sheep of his pasture. Enter his gates with thanksgiving, and his courts with praise! Give thanks to him; bless his name!
Psalm 103:1-2
Of David. Bless the Lord, O my soul, and all that is within me, bless his holy name! Bless the Lord, O my soul, and forget not all his benefits,

Our Lord is Jehovah Jireh, the Lord who provides. He is Jehovah Rapha, the Lord who heals. God is Jehovah Nissi, the Lord my banner, that is, he leads our way. I just received word that my friend is doing well and the short message he sent out was "God Is Good". In reply to his message, my response was, "All The Time". I am so grateful.

Day 24

Honor, it seems such an easy word. But what does it really mean? As a noun, it means high respect or esteem or a privilege. We as Christians are called to use it also as a verb. As a verb it means to regard with Respect and also to Fulfill (an obligation) or to Keep (an agreement).

Deuteronomy 5:16
"'Honor your father and your mother, as the Lord your God commanded you, that your days may be long, and that it may go well with you in the land that the Lord your God is giving you.
Hebrews 13:18
Pray for us, for we are sure that we have a clear conscience, desiring to act honorably in all things.
1 Timothy 5:17-18
Let the elders who rule well be considered worthy of double honor, especially those who labor in preaching and teaching. For the Scripture says, "You shall not muzzle an ox when it treads out the grain," and, "The laborer deserves his wages."
1 Timothy 1:17
To the King of ages, immortal, invisible, the only God, be honor and glory forever and ever. Amen.

According to the Bible, there is a boatload of honoring for us to do! Although most of the Bible admonishes us to act out our faith and use honor as a verb, truly the Honor is all ours to serve the one that gave all He had to Honor God the Father and grant us grace where there should have been judgement…AMEN.

Day 25

During a recent conference, a friend gave a moving talk about how his father's life changed after his heart attack. His father was overcome with the fear of dying. He was so overcome with the fear of dying that it translated into a fear of living. The Bible has something to say about that...

Hebrews 2:15
And deliver all those who through fear of death were subject to lifelong slavery.
John 10:10
The thief comes only to steal and kill and destroy. I came that they may have life and have it abundantly.
John 5:24
Truly, truly, I say to you, whoever hears my word and believes him who sent me has eternal life. He does not come into judgment, but has passed from death to life.
1 John 4:18
There is no fear in love, but perfect love casts out fear. For fear has to do with punishment, and whoever fears has not been perfected in love.

... "Who through fear of death were subject to lifelong slavery." WOW. It's true that some people fear death so much that they become slaves to the fear and no longer live life abundantly as God intended. But there is Good News! Whoever believes in Jesus passes from the fear of death to the knowing that the end of this life is the beginning of life eternal with God. Whoever knows Jesus, knows Love and perfect love casts out all fear. Focus on Jesus who is Love and cast your fears aside today so that you can truly live life to the fullest.

Day 26

Can you name someone that is more "in it" for you than you are for yourself? I can name one for you… JESUS.

Romans 8:31
What then shall we say to these things? If God is for us, who can be against us?
Joshua 1:9
Have I not commanded you? Be strong and courageous. Do not be frightened, and do not be dismayed, for the Lord your God is with you wherever you go."
Proverbs 3:5-6
Trust in the Lord with all your heart, and do not lean on your own understanding. In all your ways acknowledge him, and he will make straight your paths.
1 John 2:1
My little children, I am writing these things to you so that you may not sin. But if anyone does sin, we have an advocate with the Father, Jesus Christ the righteous.

Not only is Jesus "in it" for you, He decided to go "ALL IN" for you and sacrifice His own life so that He could advocate to the Father on your behalf. There are lots of benefits of having God on your side. Benefits like protection, strength, courage, love, grace, a peace that surpasses all understanding, and everlasting life just to name a few.

Day 27

The center of everything is peace. If you've ever had the awesome experience of having the eye of a hurricane pass directly over you, then you know that it's calm, sunny, beautiful and peaceful. Around the eye of the storm there is destruction, devastation and panic, but in the eye, there is peace.

Philippians 4:7 (AMP)
And the peace of God [that peace which reassures the heart, that peace] which transcends all understanding, [that peace which] stands guard over your hearts and your minds in Christ Jesus [is yours].
Isaiah 26:3
"The steadfast of mind You will keep in perfect peace, Because he trusts in You.
2 Thessalonians 3:16
Now may the Lord of peace himself give you peace at all times in every way. The Lord be with you all.
Psalm 107:29
He made the storm be still, and the waves of the sea were hushed.

Psalm 107:29 is told in much more detail in Luke 8:23-25. Everyone on board was panicking on the boat in the storm. Since the winds were worsening and the boat was filling with water, they woke Jesus to alert Him that they were going to die. Jesus rebuked the storm and it became Calm and Peaceful. Jesus then asked, "Where is your faith?" When the winds blow in our life and our boat is filling with water, is our response to be fearful or is our faith strong enough to provide calm and peace in the storm?

Day 28

There is a Japanese term called Wabi Sabi. Loosely translated, it is when we take something that is cracked or broken and repair it to be better than it originally was. The Bible has something to say about Wabi Sabi…

Psalm 147:3
He heals the brokenhearted and binds up their wounds.
Matthew 15:30
And great crowds came to him, bringing with them the lame, the blind, the crippled, the mute, and many others, and they put them at his feet, and he healed them,
2 Corinthians 5:17
Therefore, if anyone is in Christ, he is a new creation. The old has passed away; behold, the new has come.
1 Peter 1:23
Since you have been born again, not of perishable seed but of imperishable, through the living and abiding word of God;

God sees the beauty through the brokenness and repairs us. Through Christ, we are a new creation. When the old passes away, the new is imperishable. We aren't like the person we were before, we become much, much better than we were.

Day 29

I recently heard a great question. Do you read the Bible so that God will love you? OR, Do you read the Bible because God does love you?

Ephesians 2:8
For by grace you have been saved through faith; and that not of yourselves, it is the gift of God;
Ephesians 2:10
For we are His workmanship, created in Christ Jesus for good works, which God prepared beforehand so that we would walk in them.
Titus 3:5
He saved us, not because of works done by us in righteousness, but according to his own mercy, by the washing of regeneration and renewal of the Holy Spirit,
Matthew 4:4
But he answered, "It is written, "'Man shall not live by bread alone, but by every word that comes from the mouth of God.'"

There's nothing you can DO including reading the Bible that will make God love you. There is nothing you can DO to save your soul from separation from it's creator (truly the definition of Hell) except to Believe and have Faith in Him. Having recognized that, it is also true that Life is fed by the words contained in the Bible. So read the Bible because God loves you, not because you hope He will love you just because you read it.

Day 30

Seems people today are always hunting for a "get rich quick" scheme. The Lotto seems to be the most popular of them. So, What does the Bible say about gambling?

Mark 15:24
And they crucified Him, and divided up His garments among themselves, casting lots for them to decide what each man should take.
Proverbs 16:33
The lot is cast into the lap, but its every decision is from the Lord.
1 Timothy 6:10
For the love of money is a root of all kinds of evils. It is through this craving that some have wandered away from the faith and pierced themselves with many pangs.
Proverbs 23:5
When your eyes light on it, it is gone, for suddenly it sprouts wings, flying like an eagle toward heaven.
Proverbs 10:4
A slack hand causes poverty, but the hand of the diligent makes rich.

Biblically, sometimes gambling was in the form of a wager and that was not portrayed in a positive way. Sometimes it was in the form of a lot to make a decision but in the end, the lesson is that every decision is from God, not luck. The motive behind gambling is to win money but you can't love money and God with all your heart at the same time. The Bible teaches that even if you win, the money will "sprout wings" and leave as quickly as it arrived (often leaving you poorer in the end). And we all know the best way to become rich, trust God and use your time and talents to earn it.

How might we spend our $2 lottery money in a more biblical way?

Day 31

Without getting political, do you know how to "Make America Great Again"? Well, the answer is actually found within the pages of the Bible.

Exodus 20:3-17

3 "You shall have no other gods before me.

4 "You shall not make for yourself a carved image, or any likeness of anything that is in heaven above, or that is in the earth beneath, or that is in the water under the earth. 5 You shall not bow down to them or serve them, for I the Lord your God am a jealous God, visiting the iniquity of the fathers on the children to the third and the fourth generation of those who hate me, 6 but showing steadfast love to thousands of those who love me and keep my commandments.

7 "You shall not take the name of the Lord your God in vain, for the Lord will not hold him guiltless who takes his name in vain.

8 "Remember the Sabbath day, to keep it holy. 9 Six days you shall labor, and do all your work, 10 but the seventh day is a Sabbath to the Lord your God. On it you shall not do any work, you, or your son, or your daughter, your male servant, or your female servant, or your livestock, or the sojourner who is within your gates. 11 For in six days the Lord made heaven and earth, the sea, and all that is in them, and rested on the seventh day. Therefore the Lord blessed the Sabbath day and made it holy.

12 "Honor your father and your mother that your days may be long in the land that the Lord your God is giving you.

13 "You shall not murder.

14 "You shall not commit adultery.

15 "You shall not steal.

16 "You shall not bear false witness against your neighbor.

17 "You shall not covet your neighbor's house; you shall not covet your neighbor's wife, or his male servant, or his female servant, or his ox, or his donkey, or anything that is your neighbor's."

How is that for a start? And that's the Old Testament. There's even more advice about the same subject matter in Matthew 5:17-22 by Jesus. What would America look like if we ALL truly just followed the 10 commandments? My guess is that America would be great again. We would have no need for public leaders because we would all be public servants and we would be blessed beyond measure for giving honor and glory to God.

Day 32

Thy Will Be Done. We have uttered these words more than we can even remember in faith and in prayer. We prayed for something else and we wound up here but Thy Will Be Done. We know God is good but it doesn't feel good right now. Thy Will Be Done. It's hard to count it all joy but Thy Will Be Done.

Matthew 6:6, 9-13 (KJV)
6 But thou, when thou prayest, enter into thy closet, and when thou hast shut thy door, pray to thy Father which is in secret; and thy Father which seeth in secret shall reward thee openly.
9 After this manner therefore pray ye:
Our Father which art in heaven, Hallowed be thy name.
10 Thy kingdom come, THY WILL BE DONE in earth, as it is in heaven.
11 Give us this day our daily bread.
12 And forgive us our debts, as we forgive our debtors.
13 And lead us not into temptation, but deliver us from evil: For thine is the kingdom, and the power, and the glory, for ever. Amen.

I know you see me. I know you hear me, Lord. Thy Will Be Done. Your plans are for me. Thy Will Be Done. Goodness and Good News you have in store. Thy Will Be Done. Are we strong enough to live out what we say in faith and truly Let Thy Will Be Done? Lord help us to allow Your Will to Be Done in our lives.

Day 33

We Americans are often faced with difficult decisions. Sometimes the decisions seem impossible. In the most recent presidential elections we are not presented with the choice of picking the best person for the job. We are forced to pick the lesser of the two evils. Although both candidates may seem unworthy of the job, God has already come up with a plan to use them anyway.

Isaiah 6:5-7
5 Then I said, "Woe is me, for I am ruined! Because I am a man of unclean lips, And I live among a people of unclean lips; For my eyes have seen the King, the LORD of hosts." 6 Then one of the seraphim flew to me with a burning coal in his hand, which he had taken from the altar with tongs. 7 He touched my mouth with it and said, "Behold, this has touched your lips; and your iniquity is taken away and your sin is forgiven."
Acts 9:1, 15-19
1 Now Saul, still breathing threats and murder against the disciples of the Lord, went to the high priest 15 But the Lord said to him, "Go, for he is a chosen [g]instrument of Mine, to bear My name before the Gentiles and kings and the sons of Israel; 16 for I will show him how much he must suffer for My name's sake." 17 So Ananias departed and entered the house, and after laying his hands on him said, "Brother Saul, the Lord Jesus, who appeared to you on the road by which you were coming, has sent me so that you may regain your sight and be filled with the Holy Spirit." 18 And immediately there fell from his eyes something like scales, and he regained his sight, and he got up and was baptized; 19 and he took food and was strengthened.

Luckily, God can use ordinary people who are yet sinners to do extraordinary things in extraordinary ways. That's not just for presidential candidates, it's for us too! AMEN.

Day 34

It's easy to read the kind and loving and "soft" side of the Bible. We love to recall the stories of the Bible that many of us were taught by our parents or in Sunday school. But, as you begin to dive deeper into the Bible you will find verses that will challenge your belief. Atheists will bring up verses like 2 Kings 2:23–24 or 1 Sam 15:1 3, etc. and rush to convict God and Christians based only about the surface meaning without full context to the entirety of the Bible and without an understanding of the culture and history of the people when it was written.

2 Peter 3:16 (since the beginning of time biblical scripture was hard to understand)
as he does in all his letters when he speaks in them of these matters. There are some things in them that are hard to understand, which the ignorant and unstable twist to their own destruction, as they do the other Scriptures.
1 Peter 3:15 (always be prepared to defend the Truth)
But sanctify the Lord God in your hearts, and always be ready to give a defense to everyone who asks you a reason for the hope that is in you, with meekness and fear;

In Scripture, just as we do with difficult situations in life, we often find ourselves asking, "Why would God allow/cause/do that?" We are called to examine scripture in context and compare scripture to scripture to come up with sound biblical answers. By doing this, we can avoid falling into the trap of intentionally ignoring or denying the parts of the Bible we don't personally like and falsely accusing God of characteristics He doesn't have.

Day 35

People fear death. We spend oodles of money on vitamins, health clubs, health food, doctors, elixirs, potions and lotions all to try to avoid the inevitable. Steve Jobs was quoted before his death as saying that "No one wants to die. Even people who want to go to heaven don't want to die to get there. And yet death is the destination we all share."

Ecclesiastes 12:7
And the dust returns to the earth as it was, and the spirit returns to God who gave it.
Daniel 12:2
And many of those who sleep in the dust of the earth shall awake, some to everlasting life, and some to shame and everlasting contempt.
Psalm 23:4
Even though I walk through the valley of the shadow of death, I will fear no evil, for you are with me; your rod and your staff, they comfort me.
Revelation 21:4
He will wipe away every tear from their eyes, and death shall be no more, neither shall there be mourning, nor crying, nor pain anymore, for the former things have passed away."

I've heard it said that we are going to be really sorry about having taken all those vitamins, eating health food and for having worked out so much when we are lying in a hospital bed trying to die and we have to wait another week or two because we are too healthy to get the job done. While dying can be hard for both the person dying as well as those that love them, death is only hard for those left behind. Let us pray that we and those we love are among the elect and that our transition from this life to the life everlasting is a peaceful and beautiful experience.

Day 36

Ever wonder what the difference between magic and miracles is? Miracles are an example of God's power intervening in the world. Magic is an attempt to circumvent God in the acquisition of knowledge or power. Magic does not glorify God, but miracles do. There are many examples of magic and miracles in the Bible but I think this example from Exodus explains it best...

Exodus 7:10–12

10 So Moses and Aaron went to Pharaoh and did just as the Lord commanded. Aaron cast down his staff before Pharaoh and his servants, and it became a serpent. 11 Then Pharaoh summoned the wise men and the sorcerers, and they, the magicians of Egypt, also did the same by their secret arts. 12 For each man cast down his staff, and they became serpents. But Aaron's staff swallowed up their staffs.

Magic involves manipulation and opposition to the truth but miracles reveal the truth. Both Aaron's staff and the magician's staffs turned into snakes. When Aaron's staff consumed the staffs of the magicians it revealed the truth that no amount of magic can ever equal or defeat the power of God Almighty through His miracles. Magic distracts the mind and fools the eye. Miracles open the mind and focus our eyes on God.

Day 37

During the presidential and vice presidential debates, the candidates looked into the camera, came into the sanctity of our homes and, without blinking, blatantly lied to us. What's worse is that everyone knows this to be true and we are supposed to accept this as just "the way things are". Quite the contrary, God tells us lies and deceptions are definitely not OK, nor should they be accepted as status quo.

Proverbs 19:9
A false witness will not go unpunished, and he who breathes out lies will perish.
Revelation 21:8
But as for the cowardly, the faithless, the detestable, as for murderers, the sexually immoral, sorcerers, idolaters, and all liars, their portion will be in the lake that burns with fire and sulfur, which is the second death."
Galatians 6:7-8
Do not be deceived: God is not mocked, for whatever one sows, that will he also reap. For the one who sows to his own flesh will from the flesh reap corruption, but the one who sows to the Spirit will from the Spirit reap eternal life.
Proverbs 12:22
Lying lips are an abomination to the Lord, but those who act faithfully are his delight.

Do you know how to definitively tell the difference between the truth and a lie? Study the Truth, the incorruptible, indestructible, ever-living seed of the Word of God. And when you do this, you will know the Truth and the Truth will set you free.

Day 38

Reading the Bible is great and it will answer many questions for you. The Bible will also inspire you to think more deeply about God and help you get to know Him on a more personal level. Even though you can learn a lot by reading it on your own, even more insight will be given you when you study the Word with others.

Acts 8:27-31
And he rose and went. And there was an Ethiopian, a eunuch, a court official of Candace, queen of the Ethiopians, who was in charge of all her treasure. He had come to Jerusalem to worship and was returning, seated in his chariot, and he was reading the prophet Isaiah. And the Spirit said to Philip, "Go over and join this chariot." So Philip ran to him and heard him reading Isaiah the prophet and asked, "Do you understand what you are reading?" And he said, "How can I, unless someone guides me?" And he invited Philip to come up and sit with him.

I have been very fortunate to have studied the Bible with the same group of guys for the last 15 years or so. I am so grateful for them because just as Philip did for the Ethiopian, the guys in my study do for me. They guide me to a deeper understanding. Also, never underestimate the power of what happens when two or more gather in His name. Read the Bible and find a friend to study with you whether they be near or far.

Day 39

One of the things we Christians find most difficult is accepting compliments. It can be a humbling experience. We appreciate the compliments and find them to be an encouragement but we often feel unworthy of them. The Bible teaches us how to deal with compliments in a Christian way.

Philippians 2:8
And being found in human form, he humbled himself by becoming obedient to the point of death, even death on a cross.
James 1:17-18
Every good gift and every perfect gift is from above, coming down from the Father of lights with whom there is no variation or shadow due to change. Of his own will he brought us forth by the word of truth, that we should be a kind of first fruits of his creatures.
Romans 11:36
For from Him and through Him and to Him are all things. To Him be the glory forever! Amen.
Ephesians 3:21
to Him be the glory in the church and in Christ Jesus throughout all generations, forever and ever. Amen.

The compliments you receive are a display of Christ's love through the person complimenting you. Don't diminish the compliment; allow the light of Christ to shine back onto the person who complimented you by accepting graciously. Remember that it is only through God and Jesus that we have the ability to do what we are being complimented on. So after thanking the person for giving you the compliment, remember to give all the glory to God.

Day 40

Have you ever heard the phrase "Where the mind goes, the body follows"? Well, as it turns out, that's biblical…

Philippians 4:8
Finally, brothers, whatever is true, whatever is honorable, whatever is just, whatever is pure, whatever is lovely, whatever is commendable, if there is any excellence, if there is anything worthy of praise, think about these things.
Matthew 6:33-34
But seek first the kingdom of God and his righteousness, and all these things will be added to you. "Therefore do not be anxious about tomorrow, for tomorrow will be anxious for itself. Sufficient for the day is its own trouble.
1 Peter 5:8
Be sober-minded; be watchful. Your adversary the devil prowls around like a roaring lion, seeking someone to devour.

God admonishes us to keep our minds focused on what's important. We need to stay focused on the kingdom of God, the Truth, Justice, Grace, Purity, Love, and trying to live a sinless life even though He knows that we are prone to be tempted to sin. God reminds us to be sober-minded because we lose our focus when we are not sober. Isn't it interesting that He does not forbid us to drink alcohol, but he reminds us that the enemy is waiting in the shadows for us to be vulnerable and God forewarns us like a loving, trusting parent would do?

Day 41

Here's a challenge. Name any system of organization that does not have an intelligent designer. The fact is that there is no organized system that was not created by an intelligent designer. Think of something as simple as a birds nest. I suppose that it is possible that a wind could stir up a bunch of sticks and debris and form them into a nest and perch it perfectly on a branch in a tree but we all know that is not what happened. Intelligence, namely a bird, crafted and placed that nest in the tree.

John 1:3
All things were made through him, and without him was not any thing made that was made.
Hebrews 3:4
(For every house is built by someone, but the builder of all things is God.)
Genesis 1:1
In the beginning, God created the heavens and the earth.
Psalm 139:14
I praise you, for I am fearfully and wonderfully made. Wonderful are your works; my soul knows it very well.

If we went back in time and placed a pocket watch at the bottom of a mountain and ancient men found it, they would notice several things. That the hands both pointed up when the sun was directly above head, that the little hand went around twice in each day, that the second hand went around 60 times for each time the little hand moved to the next number, etc. But, one thing that they would never believe was that the metal and glass rolled down the mountain and somehow, by chance, formed the pocket watch working when it got to the bottom. Just as the pocket watch had an intelligent designer, so did we and the world around us. That designer was indeed God Almighty.

Day 42

In order to give us free will to choose to believe in Him through Faith, God knew that what He created also had the choice to sin and the choice not to accept Jesus as their Lord and Savior. That must have been an agonizing decision. Here is the condensed version of what happened…

Genesis 1:27
So God created man in his own image, in the image of God he created him; male and female he created them.
Proverbs 14:12
There is a way that seems right to a man, but its end is the way to death.
Romans 5:8
But God shows his love for us in that while we were still sinners, Christ died for us.
Titus 3:5
He saved us, not because of works done by us in righteousness, but according to his own mercy, by the washing of regeneration and renewal of the Holy Spirit,

Can you imagine the thoughts that go through a couple's mind when the wife is pregnant? The aspirations and hopes they have for that child but also knowing that there is a possibility that the child may get caught up in the "wrong crowd", be disobedient, maybe even become addicted to something dangerous or break the law. In the end, we have the children because of the hopes and dreams and we have faith that if something bad happens, we will have a plan to overcome it with God's mercy and grace.

Day 43

Ever heard the phrase, "If it looks too good to be true, it probably is"? The infomercial says that if you just make 3 easy payments of $19.95 you can have the DVDs with all the "Secrets" of how to loose the weight you have been carrying the last 20 years, eliminate the arthritis you have, gain muscle like Arnold Schwarzenegger or have Christie Brinkley's body. But wait! There's more! For just $9.99 (plus shipping and handling) we'll throw in the Truth…

Proverbs 19:1
Better is a poor person who walks in his integrity than one who is crooked in speech and is a fool.
Colossians 3:9
Do not lie to one another, seeing that you have put off the old self with its practices
John 8:32
And you will know the truth, and the truth will set you free."
John 14:6
Jesus said to him, "I am the way, and the truth, and the life. No one comes to the Father except through me.

And that's not all. If you ACT between NOW and before you take your last breath, God will throw in eternity in heaven at no additional cost. All of God's lines are open. Jesus is waiting to take your call. That's not just the truth, Jesus IS the TRUTH.

Day 44

There is a popular TV show that is essentially an experiment to determine what people would do when they see another person in distress or being treated badly. Some people pretend not to see the person in distress, some people see the person in need and choose not to do anything and some will intervene in some way.

Acts 20:35
In all things I have shown you that by working hard in this way we must help the weak and remember the words of the Lord Jesus, how he himself said,'It is more blessed to give than to receive.'"
Galatians 6:2
Bear one another's burdens, and so fulfill the law of Christ.
Psalm 82:4
Rescue the weak and the needy; deliver them from the hand of the wicked."
Mark 12:31
The second is this: 'You shall love your neighbor as yourself.' There is no other commandment greater than these."

Could it be that when we are tested, we would pretend to ignore or to do nothing to help? We are called to love our neighbor as ourself. Ignoring or doing nothing is a sign of apathy which is truly the opposite of love. Have our hearts become hardened and our spirits become apathetic? Let's pray. Lord Jesus, enter our hearts to soften them and renew our spirit so that we may love again as you taught us.

Day 45

Neither a borrower nor a lender be. Well, sort of…

Proverbs 22:7
The rich rules over the poor, and the borrower is the slave of the lender.
Romans 13:8
Owe no one anything, except to love each other, for the one who loves another has fulfilled the law.
Luke 6:35
But love your enemies, and do good, and lend, expecting nothing in return, and your reward will be great, and you will be sons of the Most High, for he is kind to the ungrateful and the evil.
Deuteronomy 28:12
The Lord will open to you his good treasury, the heavens, to give the rain to your land in its season and to bless all the work of your hands. And you shall lend to many nations, but you shall not borrow.

It's clear in the Bible that being a borrower is a bad thing. It will keep you in bondage to your lender. It will make you a slave. We are admonished to live within our means. But, if you read carefully, it's also not a hot idea to be a lender either. That doesn't mean never help someone out financially. Quite the contrary. The Word encourages us to Give to those that are in need without expectation of ever being repaid.

Day 46

Praying for big, huge, extraordinary blessings is a demonstration of your faith.

Philippians 4:19
And my God will supply every need of yours according to his riches in glory in Christ Jesus.
James 1:17
Every good gift and every perfect gift is from above, coming down from the Father of lights with whom there is no variation or shadow due to change.
Luke 6:38
Give, and it will be given to you. Good measure, pressed down, shaken together, running over, will be put into your lap. For with the measure you use it will be measured back to you."

BUT…Don't pray for a bigger blessing if you are going to complain about a bigger burden.

Day 47

God Is Good… All The Time!

Mark 10:17-18
"Good Teacher, what shall I do to inherit eternal life?"
"Why do you call Me good?" Jesus asked. "No one is good except God alone"
Psalm 119:68
You are good and you do good. Teach me your statutes!
Exodus 33:19
And the Lord said, "I will make all my goodness pass before your face, and I will proclaim the Lord by name before you; I will be gracious to whom I will be gracious, I will show mercy to whom I will show mercy."
Psalm 145:9
The Lord is good to all, and has compassion on all he has made
Psalm 84:11
For the Lord God is our sovereign protector. The Lord bestows favor and honor; he withholds no good thing from those who have integrity
(Genesis 1:4,10,12,18,21,25,31)
The final statement sums it up: "And God saw all that He had made, and behold, it was very good"

And All The Time…God Is Good!

Day 48

Mindfulness seems to be the buzz word of late. Secular and Western "mindfulness" seeks to calm the mind so that one can function more efficiently. Eastern philosophies such as Buddhist meditation is actually where the term came from where one is to detach themselves from suffering and empty the mind and being in the moment. Christian "mindfulness" is something quite different...

Isaiah 26:3
You keep him in perfect peace whose mind is stayed on you, because he trusts in you.
Colossians 3:2
Set your minds on things that are above, not on things that are on earth.
Colossians 2:8
See to it that no one takes you captive by philosophy and empty deceit, according to human tradition, according to the elemental spirits of the world, and not according to Christ.

Instead of following philosophies that seek to empty the mind, Christians are taught to fill the mind with one singular thing, seeking God's kingdom. Let's do as the Psalmist wrote: Test me, Lord, and try me, examine my heart and my mind; for I have always been mindful of your unfailing love and have lived in reliance on your faithfulness. – Psalm 26:2-3

Day 49

Ever been around people that sit and complain about their situation all the time? Sure, they really do have some tough things to work out but they never stop dwelling on the negatives. You sit there listening, trying to do your best to help them when you can, but after a while it becomes a drain on your spirit. What are we to do?

Philippians 4: 10-14, 19-20
10 I rejoiced in the Lord greatly that now at length you have revived your concern for me. You were indeed concerned for me, but you had no opportunity. 11 Not that I am speaking of being in need, for I have learned in whatever situation I am to be content. 12 I know how to be brought low, and I know how to abound. In any and every circumstance, I have learned the secret of facing plenty and hunger, abundance and need. 13 I can do all things through him who strengthens me. 14 Yet it was kind of you to share[f] my trouble... 19 And my God will supply every need of yours according to his riches in glory in Christ Jesus. 20 To our God and Father be glory forever and ever. Amen.

Do you hear the difference in the way the Apostle Paul describes tough times? He rejoices in the Lord even when he talks about hunger and need. He rejoices in good and in bad alike. Some people focus on the negatives, others focus on God. So, what are we to do? It is kind of you to share their trouble but the best thing you can do for them is teach our friends the "SECRET"... I can do all things through Christ who strengthens me.

Day 50

Have you noticed that the media including TV, movies, video games, music and the like are not very positive these days? What is the lead story on the news talking about? Not something positive. That's saved for the end of the broadcast if there's any time left. Movies are more increasingly filled with violence and filth. Many video games that are popular require "killing". Music is filled with potty mouth.

1 John 2:15-17
Do not love the world or the things in the world. If anyone loves the world, the love of the Father is not in him. For all that is in the world—the desires of the flesh and the desires of the eyes and pride in possessions—is not from the Father but is from the world. And the world is passing away along with its desires, but whoever does the will of God abides forever.
Romans 12:2
Do not be conformed to this world, but be transformed by the renewal of your mind, that by testing you may discern what is the will of God, what is good and acceptable and perfect.

There are so many distractions from what's important these days. If it's not the media, it's other "things" in this world that vie for our attention. Take a deep breath. Refocus. Focus on God, the Alpha and the Omega. May His Word forever be in our minds, on our lips and in our hearts to remind us to put God first place in our lives.

Day 51

Have you ever been in church and things seemed a little rushed? Almost like the priest or pastor was "hurrying things along" to get everyone out of church quickly so that they could go off and do something else? Well, tonight in church was quite the opposite. The pace of things seemed deliberately slowed down. It was as if Father Chew wanted us to more fully embrace the reverence of the moment…

Hebrews 12:28
Therefore let us be grateful for receiving a kingdom that cannot be shaken, and thus let us offer to God acceptable worship, with reverence and awe,
Exodus 3:5
Then he said, "Do not come near; take your sandals off your feet, for the place on which you are standing is holy ground."
John 20:26
Eight days later, His disciples were once again inside with the doors locked, and Thomas was with them. Jesus came and stood among them and said, "Peace be with you."

Tonight there was a palpable Reverence in the church. The doors were closed, we said the usual words, sang familiar hymns, we sat, stood and kneeled the same way we usually do but tonight, as we received communion, Jesus came and stood among us and said, "Peace be with you." May it also be with your spirit as you say your prayers today.

Day 52

Today the weather here is absolutely perfect. It truly is a gift. The weather may not be as beautiful where you are but still, you can look around and see endless gifts. The air we breathe, the food we eat, the water we drink, the gift of health, and that's not even mentioning the gifts God speaks of in the Bible…

James 1:17
Every good gift and every perfect gift is from above, coming down from the Father of lights with whom there is no variation or shadow due to change.
1 Peter 4:10
As each has received a gift, use it to serve one another, as good stewards of God's varied grace:
Ephesians 2:8-9

For by grace you have been saved through faith. And this is not your own doing; it is the gift of God, not a result of works, so that no one may boast. The gift of a Savior, Love, Grace, Peace, Purpose, Strength, Freedom, Direct Access To God through Prayer, and Hope just to name a few gifts that are available to you through God.

Day 53

"Why hasn't God answered my prayer yet?" I hear it all the time so that must be a common question. Maybe you have asked the very same question a time or two. Truth is that Persistent prayers get the attention of God so don't stop praying. Persistent prayers demonstrate true faith.

Matthew 7:7 (AMP)
"Ask and keep on asking and it will be given to you; seek and keep on seeking and you will find; knock and keep on knocking and the door will be opened to you.
Psalm 40:1
I waited patiently for the LORD; And He inclined to me and heard my cry.
Ephesians 6:18
With all prayer and petition pray at all times in the Spirit, and with this in view, be on the alert with all perseverance and petition for all the saints,
1 Thessalonians 5:17
pray without ceasing;

"Many of life's failures are people who did not realize how close to success they were when they gave up" – Thomas Edison. Persist in your prayers. You are closer to an answer than you think.

Day 54

In the movie Shadowlands, a biographical film about C.S. Lewis, C.S. Lewis' wife's health was improving following a serious illness. One of Lewis's friends said to him: "I know how hard you've been praying and now God is answering your prayers."

Jeremiah 29:12
Then you will call upon Me and come and pray to Me, and I will listen to you.
Romans 8:26-27
Likewise the Spirit helps us in our weakness. For we do not know what to pray for as we ought, but the Spirit himself intercedes for us with groanings too deep for words. And he who searches hearts knows what is the mind of the Spirit, because the Spirit intercedes for the saints according to the will of God.
1 Thessalonians 5:17
Pray without ceasing,
Philippians 4:6
Do not be anxious about anything, but in everything by prayer and supplication with thanksgiving let your requests be made known to God.

C.S. Lewis replied: "That's not why I pray. I pray because I can't help myself. I pray because I'm helpless. I pray because the need flows out of me all the time, waking and sleeping. It doesn't change God, it changes me."

Day 55

It seems as though as I grow older it's tougher and tougher to be tolerant. I find it harder to look the other way, turn the other cheek or put up with nonsense. Could it be that as we get older, it is harder and harder to be a Christian? Could it be that the test gets harder as you go along instead of easier?

Ephesians 4:2
With all humility and gentleness, with patience, bearing with one another in love,
John 8:7
And as they continued to ask him, he stood up and said to them, "Let him who is without sin among you be the first to throw a stone at her."
Exodus 14:14
The Lord will fight for you, and you have only to be silent."
Ephesians 4:1-3
I therefore, a prisoner for the Lord, urge you to walk in a manner worthy of the calling to which you have been called, with all humility and gentleness, with patience, bearing with one another in love, eager to maintain the unity of the Spirit in the bond of peace.

As you get older and more mature in your walk with Christ, you will realize being Christian will not become easier and easier; it will become harder and harder to emulate the one that walked the earth sinless. When you get a little older and a little more crotchety, and point a finger in judgment, you will look down at your hand, turn it over, and find that you have three fingers pointing right back at you. Get old, not crotchety. Judge less, love more.

Day 56

Our society has begun to call evil good, and as a result, society has begun to persecute good. Remove an "o" from 'good' in that sentence and it's still true. As the dark is getting darker, we as lights need to become brighter.

2 Timothy 3:12
Indeed, all who desire to live a godly life in Christ Jesus will be persecuted,
John 15:18
"If the world hates you, know that it has hated me before it hated you.
Matthew 5:10
"Blessed are those who are persecuted for righteousness' sake, for theirs is the kingdom of heaven.
Matthew 5:44
But I say to you, Love your enemies and pray for those who persecute you,

When you feel persecuted for doing the right and good thing, take solace in the fact that all the darkness in the world can not overcome the light of a single candle. It's tempting to "go with the crowd" and join in when your friends and family are doing things that look "fun" even though you know those things go against God's will. Instead of becoming one of the "sheeple" following the crowd, be the light that brightens a dark corner of this world.

Day 57

Sometimes it's not what you know…it's who you know. Have you ever seen someone get a promotion or some other type of favor in their lives and you didn't think they deserved it? You thought it was just who they knew that got them where they are. You felt it wasn't fair didn't you?

Psalm 46:10
"Cease striving and know that I am God; I will be exalted among the nations, I will be exalted in the earth."
Ephesians 2:8-9
For by grace you have been saved through faith; and that not of yourselves, it is the gift of God; not as a result of works, so that no one may boast.
Ephesians 2:5
even when we were dead in our transgressions, made us alive together with Christ (by grace you have been saved),

Ever stop and wonder how you got saved from eternal damnation? It was through the blood and sacrifice of Jesus Christ. Your salvation was a gift, through grace. We didn't deserve it but still, we got it. It wasn't what we know ourselves, it is completely based on who we know to be the Son of God. It wasn't fair. It was Amazing Grace.

Day 58

Why is it that we are attracted to things that are forbidden? Our human nature causes us to want what we can not have. We know what's right and what's wrong but we are drawn in by our EGO (which stands for Edging God Out). Listen in as God reveals in His Word how man was deceived into doing what was forbidden for the very first time in history…

Genesis 2:17
but from the tree of the knowledge of good and evil you shall not eat, for in the day that you eat from it you will surely die."
Genesis 3:1
[The Fall of Man] Now the serpent was craftier than any beast of the field which the Lord God had made. And he said to the woman, "Indeed, has God said, 'You shall not eat from any tree of the garden'?"

Deception and doubt are used by the enemy. The devil asked Eve, "Did God really say you shall not eat from the tree?" Reduced by deception and doubt, Eve succumbs to temptation. What "fruit" have you been tempted by? Stay focused on God and the Word so that when the liar and deceiver attempts to deceive you, there will be no doubt what the right thing to do will be. May God bless you with the strength to overcome temptation and avoid what is forbidden.

Day 59

When you ask most people what they most desire, the most common answer is Peace and happiness. This world and all the evil within it attempts to rob us of that which we desire most. Jesus knew that and he left us with an incredible gift.

John 14:27
Peace I leave with you; My peace I give to you; not as the world gives do I give to you. Do not let your heart be troubled, nor let it be fearful.
Luke 2:14
"Glory to God in the highest, And on earth peace among men with whom He is pleased."
Luke 10:5
Whatever house you enter, first say, 'Peace be to this house.'

Even when we are confronted with things that seek to rob us of peace and happiness, know that God is with you and He wants you to accept His gift. Glory to God in the highest and on earth PEACE to good people of good will.

Day 60

Are you new to Christianity or have you recently (or maybe not so recently) asked Jesus into your heart and you just don't feel the love yet? Maybe that empty place you thought that Jesus would fill still feels a little bit…empty? Well, as it turns out, you're not alone.

1 John 4:10
In this is love, not that we loved God, but that He loved us.
Acts 17:27
So that they should seek the Lord, in the hope that they might grope for Him and find Him, though He is not far from each one of us.
Hebrews 13:5
I will never leave you nor forsake you.

Developing a loving relationship takes time. It takes prayer, reading the Word of God and meditating on it to develop the intimacy that will grow over time. Even Jesus took time alone to pray and grow his relationship with God. We wouldn't expect to have just met someone and all of a sudden have a deep meaningful love and relationship and get married in a few days. Sometimes developing a meaningful relationship and a true, deep, agape love takes years. It's no different with our relationship with God through Jesus.

Day 61

Before Jesus, in the Old Testament, each year the Jewish people had to bring a Pure, Spotless animal to the high priest to be used as a sacrifice for their sins. It was a stressful time for the priest and the person bringing the animal. What if the sacrifice wasn't Pure enough or Spotless enough? Even if it was the perfect sacrifice, it couldn't forgive their sins, it would only Cover their sins for another year...

Romans 10:9
Because, if you confess with your mouth that Jesus is Lord and believe in your heart that God raised him from the dead, you will be saved.
Ephesians 2:8-9
For by grace you have been saved through faith. And this is not your own doing; it is the gift of God, not a result of works, so that no one may boast.
John 3:16
"For God so loved the world, that he gave his only Son, that whoever believes in him should not perish but have eternal life.

For those that believe in Jesus, the Christ, our sins are not covered, they are forgiven. They are not forgiven for a year, they are forgiven forever. We don't need to stress out about whether our sacrifice was good enough; Jesus made the ultimate sacrifice for us. We are forgiven, now go and sin no more...(or do the very best you can to try not to).

Day 62

How about something a little lighter for today? Are dinosaurs mentioned in the Bible? Well, the jury is out on that one. The Bible does mention the Hebrew word תַּנִּין tannîyn, tan-neen'; or תַּנִּים tannîym which is literally translated as sea monster, serpent or dragon. In Job, The behemoth is said to be the mightiest of all God's creatures, a giant whose tail is likened to a cedar tree.

Job 40:15-24
Behold now behemoth, which I made with thee; he eateth grass as an ox.
Ezekiel 29:3
Speak, and say, Thus saith the Lord God; Behold, I am against thee, Pharaoh king of Egypt, the great dragon that lieth in the midst of his rivers, which hath said, My river is mine own, and I have made it for myself.

So, it's your call. Are dinosaurs mentioned in the Bible? It depends on you interpretation of the evidences and how you understand the world around you. It is interesting that the Hebrew תַּנִּין (tanniyn), appears 28 times in 28 verses in the Hebrew concordance of the KJV. Check out a few of those references and decide for yourself.

Day 63

Have you ever heard the phrase, "God would never give you more than you can handle?" Turns out, that's not exactly true. When it comes to temptation and sin, it is absolutely 100% true. But when it comes to suffering, it's not true at all. In fact, even Jesus came to a point where He felt that He had been given more than he could handle.

1 Corinthians 10:13
"No temptation has overtaken you except what is common to mankind. And God is faithful; He will not let you be tempted beyond what you can bear. But when you are tempted, He will also provide a way out so that you can endure it"
Matthew 26:38
The night before Jesus was crucified, He cried out to God, "My soul is overwhelmed with sorrow to the point of death".

Psalm 22 and 88 cry out to God respectively:
"Why have you forsaken me?" and "darkness is my closest friend"
Even Jesus told His Father, "This is too much for me!" It's OK to cry out, "My soul is overwhelmed with sorrow to the point of death." When we do this, we truly find and rely on God, the one that became human in the person of Jesus to suffer for us and with us. When we admit that life can truly dish up much more than we can handle, God is faithful to meet us in the chaos and pain to suffer with us until we are ready for Him to show us the way to move forward.

Day 64

The story of Daniel is one that hits close to home for many of us. You see, there was a law against praying to anyone but the king. Not only did Daniel continue to pray to God but he did it openly in front of his enemies and they turned him in for breaking the law; the penalty for which was being thrown into a pit of lions…

Daniel 6 (NLT)

3 Daniel soon proved himself more capable than all the other administrators and high officers. Because of Daniel's great ability, the king made plans to place him over the entire empire.

7 We are all in agreement—we administrators, officials, high officers, advisers, and governors—that the king should make a law that will be strictly enforced. Give orders that for the next thirty days any person who prays to anyone, divine or human—except to you, Your Majesty—will be thrown into the den of lions

10 But when Daniel learned that the law had been signed, he went home and knelt down as usual in his upstairs room, with its windows open toward Jerusalem. He prayed three times a day, just as he had always done, giving thanks to his God.

16 So at last the king gave orders for Daniel to be arrested and thrown into the den of lions. The king said to him, "May your God, whom you serve so faithfully, rescue you."

19 Very early the next morning, the king got up and hurried out to the lions' den. 20 When he got there, he called out in anguish, "Daniel, servant of the living God! Was your God, whom you serve so faithfully, able to rescue you from the lions?"

23 The king was overjoyed and ordered that Daniel be lifted from the den. Not a scratch was found on him, for he had trusted in his God.

What are we to make of this story today? What would you have done? Would you have prayed openly when you knew the sentence for this "crime"? What will you do next time you are out to dinner and you're with people that don't pray before they eat? Maybe they're not Christians, or perhaps they are atheists. Would you still pray? Would you pause with hands clasped or head bowed to thank God for the food before you? Or will you hide your faith or maybe pray secretly so no one will know? Be courageous in your faith.

Day 65

PUNCTUALITY: Showing respect for other people by respectfully using the limited time they have. The late great football coach, Vince Lombardi said, "If you are five minutes early, you are already ten minutes late."

Proverbs 12:27
Whoever is slothful will not roast his game, but the diligent man will get precious wealth.
Luke 13:25
When the master of the house has locked the door, it will be too late. You will stand outside knocking and pleading, 'Lord, open the door for us!' But he will reply, 'I don't know you or where you come from.'
Luke 19:42
"How I wish today that you of all people would understand the way to peace. But now it is too late, and peace is hidden from your eyes.
Romans 13:11
This is all the more urgent, for you know how late it is; time is running out. Wake up, for our salvation is nearer now than when we first believed.

Being on time often isn't good enough. When we plan to be early and anticipate the inevitable hold up that will slow us down, it shows other people that we respect their most valued commodity…Time. Time is truly the best gift you can give someone because you arc giving them something you can never get back.

Day 66

Jesus is known as the Good Shepherd. We should also admonish ourselves to exhibit the qualities of a shepherd…they are guardians, they are committed, they are dedicated, they are humble, they are dependant upon God, they have a servant's heart, they demonstrate endurance, and they are willing to pursue in the face of danger to save even one of their flock.

1 Corinthians 15:58
Therefore, my beloved brothers, be steadfast, immovable, always abounding in the work of the Lord, knowing that in the Lord your labor is not in vain.
John 6:38-39
For I have come down from heaven, not to do My own will, but to do the will of Him who sent Me. And this is the will of Him who sent Me, that I shall lose none of all those He has given Me, but raise them up at the last day.
John 17:12
During my time here, I protected them by the power of the name you gave me. I guarded them so that not one was lost, except the one headed for destruction, as the Scriptures foretold.
Luke 15:4
"If a man has a hundred sheep and one of them gets lost, what will he do? Won't he leave the ninety-nine others in the wilderness and go to search for the one that is lost until he finds it?

Do you know how you can tell that you really love someone? You would be willing to pursue them in the face of danger. No matter how badly the odds seem to be stacked against you, with endurance, you continue share the Good News with them. Who do you know that's worth pursuing with love, dedication, humility, and a servant's heart in an effort to lead them to God?

Day 67

I've heard that public speaking is one of the most common fears that people have. Interesting that the Great Commission is to go out and TELL the whole world about the Gospel of Jesus Christ.

Colossians 4:6
Let your speech always be gracious, seasoned with salt, so that you may know how you ought to answer each person.
Luke 12:11-12
And when they bring you before the synagogues and the rulers and the authorities, do not be anxious about how you should defend yourself or what you should say, for the Holy Spirit will teach you in that very hour what you ought to say."
Exodus 4:12
Now therefore go, and I will be with your mouth and teach you what you shall speak."
Ephesians 6:19-20
And also for me, that words may be given to me in opening my mouth boldly to proclaim the mystery of the gospel, for which I am an ambassador in chains, that I may declare it boldly, as I ought to speak.

You don't need to know chapter and verse of the Bible to share your faith. Don't be worried that you won't "say the right thing" or that you will "embarrass yourself". Know that God will provide the right words for you at the right time in the right place if you will just be willing to stand in faith and open your mouth boldly. OK, well that doesn't sound as scary any more. Its Time to Go out and Proclaim the Good News!

Day 68

Ever read Aesop's fable about the grasshopper and the ants? Well, the grasshopper decided to play and just enjoy the summer. The ants, however, decided to plan ahead for the winter by working hard during the summer and storing up food.

Proverbs 16:9
The heart of man plans his way, but the Lord establishes his steps.
2 Corinthians 9:6
The point is this: whoever sows sparingly will also reap sparingly, and whoever sows bountifully will also reap bountifully.
Proverbs 24:27
Prepare your work outside; get everything ready for yourself in the field, and after that build your house.
Proverbs 21:5
The plans of the diligent lead surely to abundance, but everyone who is hasty comes only to poverty.

The Bible is clear about planning ahead. We're not to wait until the last minute to do important things. What have you been putting off until later? What have you been thinking about and were waiting to "get around to it" but it never happened? Let's break out the to-do list and start checking things off as we get them done today. #1, 2 & 3 on my list are done...read the Bible, write about what I learned and pray...check, check and check.

Day 69

Seems our culture tries to convince us that we should be leaders. Somehow we have been fooled into believing that followers are weak and leaders are strong. We have been left with a society with too many "chiefs and not enough Indians".

1 Peter 2:21
For to this you have been called, because Christ also suffered for you, leaving you an example, so that you might follow in his steps.
Matthew 16:24
Then Jesus told his disciples, "If anyone would come after me, let him deny himself and take up his cross and follow me.
Proverbs 8:32
"And so, my children, listen to me, for all who follow my ways are joyful.
Mark 10:21
Looking at the man, Jesus felt genuine love for him. "There is still one thing you haven't done," he told him. "Go and sell all your possessions and give the money to the poor, and you will have treasure in heaven. Then come, follow me."

We are admonished to be followers of God and of Jesus in the Bible. There is nothing weak about being a follower, it takes strength to be a follower. What sounds easier: sitting on your couch watching TV eating Bon Bons or selling all your stuff and giving the proceeds to the poor to end suffering? If being a follower of Jesus was easy, everyone would follow Him. But the truth is that it is hard, nearly impossible to follow in His footsteps. The reward for trying your best to be a follower, however, is utter and complete Joy…not to mention a few other perks.

Day 70

Life is much better when we stay "in the Word". We've heard that lots of times when we've been in church but finding the time every day to read the Bible and to pray takes a lot of time, preparation and effort... Or does it?

Psalm 119:9
How can a young man keep his way pure? By guarding it according to your word.
2 Peter 3:8
But do not overlook this one fact, beloved, that with the Lord one day is as a thousand years, and a thousand years as one day.
James 4:13-15
Come now, you who say, "Today or tomorrow we will go into such and such a town and spend a year there and trade and make a profit"— yet you do not know what tomorrow will bring. What is your life? For you are a mist that appears for a little time and then vanishes. Instead you ought to say, "If the Lord wills, we will live and do this or that."
Ephesians 5:16
Making the best use of the time, because the days are evil.

Time is our most valued and scarcest commodity today but we need to prioritize our time and manage it better to get the most important things in. God needs to be at the top of our "to do" list. When we consistently put Him first, miraculously, there is more time for the other things in our lives. Take a minute each day to read a scripture from the Bible, reflect on it for a minute and they pray to God, the author of what you just read. See how your days go after making that a habit...

Day 71

In our lives we will experience periods of drought and possibly even famine. There will be times when we feel our situation is desperate and there seems no way out. Fear may even overtake us. But, if we keep God in first place and put our faith in Him, Hope comforts us.

Jeremiah 17:7-8
"Blessed is the man who trusts in the Lord, whose trust is the Lord. He is like a tree planted by water, that sends out its roots by the stream, and does not fear when heat comes, for its leaves remain green, and is not anxious in the year of drought, for it does not cease to bear fruit."
Amos 8:11
"Behold, the days are coming," declares the Lord God, "when I will send a famine on the land— not a famine of bread, nor a thirst for water, but of hearing the words of the Lord.
Psalm 119:114
You are my hiding place and my shield; I hope in your word.
Romans 5:3-5
More than that, we rejoice in our sufferings, knowing that suffering produces endurance, and endurance produces character, and character produces hope, and hope does not put us to shame, because God's love has been poured into our hearts through the Holy Spirit who has been given to us.

If we focus on God and maintain our faith, even when suffering through the times of "drought" and "famine" in our lives, Hope will see us through. Knowing that everything is going to be OK and has been worked out before the very foundation of time allows us to rejoice even in our times of suffering. Dear Lord, thank you for pouring your Love into our hearts and giving us peace in times of fear and light in times of darkness.

Day 72

What is it about a newborn that is so undeniably attractive? What is it about this New Life that draws us in to take a closer look?

Genesis 2:7
Then the Lord God formed the man of dust from the ground and breathed into his nostrils the breath of life, and the man became a living creature.
Psalm 127:3
Behold, children are a heritage from the Lord, the fruit of the womb a reward.
John 3:4-7
Nicodemus said to him, "How can a man be born when he is old? Can he enter a second time into his mother's womb and be born?" Jesus answered, "Truly, truly, I say to you, unless one is born of water and the Spirit, he cannot enter the kingdom of God. That which is born of the flesh is flesh, and that which is born of the Spirit is spirit. Do not marvel that I said to you, 'You must be born again.'

Is it that the life before is so new that it still contains the breath of God which is so attractive? Could it be the fact that the baby before us represents the reward or blessing of God that is so appealing? OR, could it be that a baby represents being born of flesh and it causes us to remember our second birth, when we were born of the Spirit, which gives us life everlasting? Our second birth is truly our gift and our reward and our blessing from God.

Day 73

"Our calendar is split between BC and AD based on the birth of Jesus which is quite a feat if he never existed. Historian Gary Habermas lists 39 separate sources for the existence of Jesus from non-Christian sources which enumerate over 100 confirmed facts about his life, teaching, crucifixion, death and resurrection. The historical facts of Jesus' execution are so strong, that one of the leading New Testament scholars, Gerd Ludemann said that Jesus' death as a consequence of crucifixion is indisputable. The interesting fact is that Gerd Ludemann is an Atheist"- Lee Strobel from the movie God's Not Dead 2

John 20:25, 27-29
"I won't believe it unless I see the nail wounds in his hands, put my fingers into them, and place my hand into the wound in his side."... Then he said to Thomas, "Put your finger here, and look at my hands. Put your hand into the wound in my side. Don't be faithless any longer. Believe!" "My Lord and my God!" Thomas exclaimed. Then Jesus told him, "You believe because you have seen me. Blessed are those who believe without seeing me."

As the agnostic historian, Bart Ehrman says, "Jesus did exist whether we like it or not." "Denying the existence of Jesus doesn't make Him go away, it merely proves that no amount of evidence could ever convince you."- Lee Strobel. As the movie points out, often there is deafening silence from Jesus and God when we are struggling. The silence may be there even as we struggle with whether or not Jesus is real. But, we must remember that during any test, the teacher is always silent.

Day 74

Good service is hard to find these days. Have you ever been out to dinner and the waiter was not attentive? I mean, they eventually got the food to the table but they left the dirty appetizer plate on the table throughout the entire meal, they were not around to ask if you needed anything so you just "made do" with what you had but really could have used that extra napkin, a lemon, more water and another bottle of ketchup. It was hard to even justify a 15% tip…

Colossians 3:23 (AMP)
23 Whatever you do [whatever your task may be], work from the soul [that is, put in your very best effort], as [something done] for the Lord and not for men,

Ever been to a restaurant and the waiters walked around with a smile and seemed to predict what you needed, having it there before you even asked? Somehow the food tasted better and we cheerfully left a tip that was over 20%. Here's another tip: Whatever our work may be, waiter, doctor, sales clerk, pastor, excavator, etc… serve those in front of you as if you were serving the Lord God, Jesus Christ Himself.

Day 75

Praise. It costs nothing but it's priceless. How does it make you feel when someone praises you or when someone speaks kind words about you to someone else?

Psalm 150:1-6
Praise the Lord! Praise God in his sanctuary; praise him in his mighty heavens! Praise him for his mighty deeds; praise him according to his excellent greatness! Praise him with trumpet sound; praise him with lute and harp! Praise him with tambourine and dance; praise him with strings and pipe! Praise him with sounding cymbals; praise him with loud clashing cymbals! ...
1 Thessalonians 5:11
Therefore encourage one another and build one another up, just as you are doing.

It's important to speak words of praise over those we love. Tell your spouse something specific that you admire and appreciate in them. Tell your kids how proud of them you are (no matter what their age). Call your parents and tell them how grateful you are. Call your siblings and praise them for something you have noticed about them. Do this with the people who work for or with you and your friends. But don't stop there! Give Praise daily, continually and sincerely to God by speaking to Him quietly in prayer or by making a Joyful noise.

Day 76

Most people struggle with the prospect of being promoted to a managerial position or with having to be the leader on a project. The fact of the matter is that you would not have been chosen for the job by your work, organization or even by God had you not been prepared to succeed as a leader.

1 Timothy 4:12
Let no one despise you for your youth, but set the believers an example in speech, in conduct, in love, in faith, in purity.
Philippians 2:3
Do nothing from rivalry or conceit, but in humility count others more significant than yourselves.
Jeremiah 23:1
"Woe to the shepherds who destroy and scatter the sheep of my pasture!" declares the Lord.
Proverbs 11:14
Where there is no guidance, a people falls, but in an abundance of counselors there is safety.

When the opportunity arises to become a leader, rise to the occasion! Lead by example. Lead with Biblical principles and conduct yourself with clean speech, love, faith, honesty, fairness, congruency and a desire to help others succeed.

Day 77

I'm sure technology including the cell phone and computer have done some good for the world but have they helped humanity? It seems as though people are looking down at their phone texting instead of looking each other in the eyes and having a meaningful conversation. Could it be we are losing the art of communication through conversation...

Colossians 4:6
Let your speech always be with grace, as though seasoned with salt, so that you will know how you should respond to each person.
Ephesians 4:29
Let no unwholesome word proceed from your mouth, but only such a word as is good for edification according to the need of the moment, so that it will give grace to those who hear.
Genesis 45:15
He kissed all his brothers and wept on them, and afterward his brothers talked with him.
Luke 24:14-15
And they were talking with each other about all these things which had taken place. While they were talking and discussing, Jesus Himself approached and began traveling with them.

The Bible is really just the communication between God and His people. It is God communicating with YOU through the Living Word contained in the Bible. Put down your phone, turn off your computer and sit down today and have a meaningful conversation with someone you truly care about. Perhaps as you are talking, Jesus Himself will approach and begin traveling with you too.

Day 78

What does the Bible say about "Good Manners"? Our men's Bible study meets at a restaurant every Thursday morning where the reply to Thank You is "My Pleasure". So simple to just reply "My Pleasure" to Thank You but it is music to our ears...

Luke 6:31
And as you wish that others would do to you, do so to them.
1 Corinthians 15:33
Do not be deceived: "Bad company ruins good morals."
1 Peter 3:8
Finally, all of you, have unity of mind, sympathy, brotherly love, a tender heart, and a humble mind.
Ephesians 4:29
Let no corrupting talk come out of your mouths, but only such as is good for building up, as fits the occasion, that it may give grace to those who hear.

There are many Bible passages that talk about kindness, love and consideration of others.

Seems we are seeing less and less good manners being used these days. Please and Thank You are so easy to use. Let's strive to become shining examples today and treat everyone with the golden rule from Luke above.

Day 79

At the core of our being, we desire to be useful, to be needed and to do good and great works with our lives. In order for God to use us to do those great works, we need to become clean, empty, willing and available vessels...

CLEAN: Therefore, if anyone cleanses himself from what is dishonorable, he will be a vessel for honorable use, set apart as holy, useful to the master of the house, ready for every good work. (2 Timothy 2:21)
"above reproach, the husband of one wife, temperate, prudent, respectable, hospitable, able to teach, not addicted to wine or pugnacious, but gentle, peaceable, free from the love of money." (1 Timothy 3: 1-3)

EMPTY: Let us throw off everything that hinders and the sin that so easily entangles. And let us run with perseverance the race marked out for us, fixing our eyes on Jesus, the pioneer and perfecter of faith. (Hebrew 12:1-2)

WILLING: Each of you should give what you have decided in your heart to give, not reluctantly or under compulsion, for God loves a cheerful giver. (2 Corinthians 9:79)

AVAILABLE: Come near to God and he will come near to you. (James 4:8)
Become a Clean, Empty, Willing and Available vessel. Let's work on preparing ourselves to be used by the Author of our lives and the Creator of the Universe so that He can do great things through us.

Day 80

Praying for others is called Intercessory Prayer. God doesn't just want us to pray for others, He commands it. In fact, when Jesus was about to be taken captive and sent to His death, He not only prayed for Himself, He prayed for His disciples and for US!

Luke 22:41-42
And He withdrew from them about a stone's throw, and He knelt down and began to pray, saying, "Father, if You are willing, remove this cup from Me; yet not My will, but Yours be done."
John 17:18-21
"I do not pray for these alone, but also for those who will believe in Me through their word; that they all may be one, as You, Father, are in Me, and I in You; that they also may be one in Us, that the world may believe that You sent Me".
1 Timothy 2:1-2
I exhort therefore, that, first of all, supplications, prayers, intercessions, and giving of thanks, be made for all men; For kings, and for all that are in authority; that we may lead a quiet and peaceable life in all godliness and honesty.

If you knew you were going to be violently taken away to your death, what would be going on in your mind? Isn't it amazing to know what was on Jesus' mind when that happened to Him? And still, His prayers were intercessory for US. Take the time today to pray for yourself, those you love and also for "those that spitefully use you and persecute you". Pray from the heart, pray often, and pray with faith, love and fervency.

Day 81

Boy Scouts are definitely on the right path. Their motto is "always be prepared". As it turns out, that's a theme found in dozens of Bible passages as well.

Matthew 24:44
Therefore you also must be ready, for the Son of Man is coming at an hour you do not expect.
1 Corinthians 16:13
Be watchful, stand firm in the faith, act like men, be strong.
Proverbs 6:6-8
Go to the ant, O sluggard; consider her ways, and be wise. Without having any chief, officer, or ruler, she prepares her bread in summer and gathers her food in harvest.
Matthew 25:13
Watch therefore, for you know neither the day nor the hour.

We know not the year, the month, the day or the hour but what we do know is that Jesus will return. When He does return, you don't want to be caught with your pants down, your guard down, or weighed down by doubt, disbelief or fears. Instead, do like the Boy Scouts do... Always be prepared.

Day 82

We are constantly being bombarded with messages that we "need" the newest and best "stuff". Our human fleshy bodies are constantly looking over the fence and wondering why the grass is always greener on the other side. We don't take enough time to consider how very grateful we should be with what we have and be Content and at peace.

Philippians 4:11-13
Not that I am speaking of being in need, for I have learned in whatever situation I am to be content. I know how to be brought low, and I know how to abound. In any and every circumstance, I have learned the secret of facing plenty and hunger, abundance and need. I can do all things through him who strengthens me.
Hebrews 13:5
Keep your life free from love of money, and be content with what you have, for he has said, "I will never leave you nor forsake you."
1 Timothy 6:6-8
Now there is great gain in godliness with contentment, for we brought nothing into the world, and we cannot take anything out of the world. But if we have food and clothing, with these we will be content.

What does it mean to be Content? Just repeat that word to yourself...Content. I am completely Content. How freeing and peaceful it is to be completely and totally content. Ask yourself, "How much is enough?" You will come to the conclusion that with God, we have more than we need.

Day 83

If we observe the world around us that God created, things that are healthy and alive are in motion, are soft and supple. Things that are dried up, brittle and stiff tend not to be as healthy and as full of life.

Acts 7:51
"You stiff-necked people, uncircumcised in heart and ears, you always resist the Holy Spirit. As your fathers did, so do you.
Exodus 32:9
And the Lord said to Moses, "I have seen this people, and behold, it is a stiff-necked people.
Jeremiah 17:23
Yet they did not listen or incline their ear, but stiffened their neck, that they might not hear and receive instruction.
Proverbs 29:1
He who is often reproved, yet stiffens his neck, will suddenly be broken beyond healing.

Being "stiff-necked" is another way of saying "stubborn". If God speaks to us through the Holy Spirit in the form of His Word in the Bible, a thought flash or just a feeling in your gut and we choose to ignore it, we have become stiff-necked. If we ignore God's offer through Jesus of eternal life with Him, we (by default) choose to become stiff, dried up, brittle and susceptible to being broken beyond repair. Choose Life.

Day 84

On our way to our goals in life, be they material or spiritual, we often lose our focus. We take our eyes off the ball, so to speak…

Proverbs 16:3
Commit your work to the Lord, and your plans will be established.
Matthew 24:13
But the one who endures to the end will be saved.
Romans 12:21
Do not be overcome by evil, but overcome evil with good.

There are so many distractions in this world. These distractions take our focus away from what we know to be right and just and true. I was once told that the most difficult place to meditate or pray is in the middle of a busy marketplace. Imagine being able to meditate and pray in the entrance way of Wal-Mart during the Christmas door buster sales hours. It may seem impossible but with God, time and repetition, you can build your "focus muscles" and overcome any obstacle that comes your way.

Day 85

What do you buy the guy or gal that "has everything"? They have enough resources to satisfy any desire of the flesh they choose. That's a daunting task but what's even tougher is satisfying the deepest desire of the heart...

Psalm 37:4
Delight yourself in the Lord, and he will give you the desires of your heart.
Matthew 6:21
For where your treasure is, there your heart will be also.
Matthew 6:33
But seek first the kingdom of God and his righteousness, and all these things will be added to you.
Romans 10:1
Brothers, my heart's desire and prayer to God for them is that they may be saved.

My wife and I have been financially poor where we lived on food stamps and were grateful for the blocks of government cheese. We have been financially rich where we lived for weeks at the Ritz Carlton on extravagant vacations. BUT, we have never been as wealthy as we are now that we focus our time and talents on serving God and our Lord and Savior Jesus. No amount of money can fill the empty void in our heart where God belongs. Ask Jesus to come into your heart today.

Day 86

You can't go anywhere without hearing about the evils in this world. Some of the evils can hit very close to home but there is safety and protection for those that put their trust and faith in the Lord.

Psalm 121
I will lift up my eyes to the mountains; From where shall my help come? 2 My help comes from the LORD, Who made heaven and earth. 3 He will not allow your foot to slip; He who keeps you will not slumber. 4 Behold, He who keeps Israel Will neither slumber nor sleep. 5 The LORD is your keeper; The LORD is your shade on your right hand. 6 The sun will not smite you by day, Nor the moon by night. 7 The LORD will protect you from all evil; He will keep your soul. 8 The LORD will guard your going out and your coming in From this time forth and forever.

WOW, there really isn't anything to say, or for that matter, anything to fear but fear itself.

What do you most fear?

Day 87

UHHHHH….. INSOMNIA... such a bummer!!! Stress levels are on the rise and the mind seems never to have a time to rest. When I have trouble sleeping, I like to just lay on my back in bed and pray…

Proverbs 3:24
If you lie down, you will not be afraid; when you lie down, your sleep will be sweet.
Psalm 4:8
In peace I will both lie down and sleep; for you alone, O Lord, make me dwell in safety.
Psalm 127:2
It is in vain that you rise up early and go late to rest, eating the bread of anxious toil; for he gives to his beloved sleep.
Proverbs 6:10
A little sleep, a little slumber, a little folding of the hands to rest,

Trouble sleeping, we've all been there. So next time that happens, do as it says in Proverbs, fold your hands, pray deeply, fully and thoroughly. Share your thoughts, concerns and desires with God. And then, keep your hands folded and just wait silently as He answers your prayers in the form of peace, love, safety, calm, and if it is His will, a little sleep and a little slumber.

Day 88

om•nip•o•tent ˌämˈnipəd(ə)nt/ adjective 1. (of a deity) having unlimited power; able to do anything.

Colossians 1:16
For by him all things were created, in heaven and on earth, visible and invisible, whether thrones or dominions or rulers or authorities—all things were created through him and for him.
John 1:1
In the beginning was the Word, and the Word was with God, and the Word was God.

WOW…OMNIPOTENT… If we are in God and God is in us, there is nothing that is beyond our ability with Him. With that in mind, if you could do ANYTHING and you knew you could not fail, what would you do? Let's give that some thought today. Maybe we have been serving those around us with a little less than omnipotence.

Day 89

Kinda, but not really… Cold, but not hot, but not really cold either… Looks like Salt, but not really salty…

Revelation 3:15-16
"'I know your works: you are neither cold nor hot. Would that you were either cold or hot! So, because you are lukewarm, and neither hot nor cold, I will spit you out of my mouth.
Matthew 5:13
"You are the salt of the earth, but if salt has lost its taste, how shall its saltiness be restored? It is no longer good for anything except to be thrown out and trampled under people's feet.

God is not looking for Kinda-Sorta. God is looking for All-In. If you are lukewarm, He says he will spit you out. Even if you look like salt, you're not going to do much good for Him and His kingdom if you have lost your saltiness. If you feel like you have gotten "cold" in your faith, allow your relationship with God to get "hot" again through a simple quiet prayer right now. Become the salt of the earth by growing closer to Him again.

What things in your life do you feel pull you away from Him?

Day 90

What is the value of an education? Some of us got our education in school while others got it through experience, apprenticeship and hard work. Some people get an education but never overlook the importance of obtaining wisdom…

Ecclesiastes 7:12
For the protection of wisdom is like the protection of money, and the advantage of knowledge is that wisdom preserves the life of him who has it.
Proverbs 16:16
How much better to get wisdom than gold! To get understanding is to be chosen rather than silver.
Proverbs 4:13
Keep hold of instruction; do not let go; guard her, for she is your life.

When the wisest man to have ever lived was asked by God what he most wanted, he did not ask for a long life or riches. He asked for a wise and discerning heart. May we never allow school to get in the way of us receiving an education and let us not confuse our education with the wisdom that can be learned from those who have gone before us. An education is valuable, wisdom is priceless.

Day 91

Bit (noun) meaning: a mouthpiece, typically made of metal, that is attached to a bridle and used to control a horse. The bit of a bridle is a very interesting thing indeed; for whomever controls the mouth, controls the entire animal.

Ephesians 4:29
Let no corrupting talk come out of your mouths, but only such as is good for building up, as fits the occasion, that it may give grace to those who hear.
Proverbs 18:21
Death and life are in the power of the tongue, and those who love it will eat its fruits.
Proverbs 17:27
Whoever restrains his words has knowledge, and he who has a cool spirit is a man of understanding.
Psalm 141:3
Set a guard over my mouth, LORD; keep watch over the door of my lips.

Don't invite the enemy to put a bit in your mouth; for if he controls your mouth, he controls you. What has been coming out of your mouth lately? If it's not words of praise, encouragement, prayer and positivity, spit out the bit

Day 92

My friend told me about a conversation he had with a professed atheist. The Atheist asked him why he believed in Christianity. My friend asked the atheist, "Tell me what happens if I'm wrong and you're right. We live our lives and when we die, it's over. The lights go out and that's it." He went on to ask, "But what if Christians are right? If we're right, and you're not saved, where will you wind up?"

Ephesians 2:8-9
For by grace you have been saved through faith. And this is not your own doing; it is the gift of God, not a result of works, so that no one may boast.
John 3:16
"For God so loved the world, that he gave his only Son, that whoever believes in him should not perish but have eternal life.
Mark 16:16
Whoever believes and is baptized will be saved, but whoever does not believe will be condemned.

Let's just assume for a minute that the Bible is the Word of God, the Good News and the Truth. Here's what happens: You live a good life in service to God, following His commandments, falling short from time to time but when you die you are given grace through your Faith and belief in Jesus Christ and you get to live for eternity with your Father in heaven. That's not a bad deal!

Day 93

Death and dying are two of the hardest topics for me. I suppose that they are for most people. As someone that is absolutely sure about God's promise of everlasting life, I'm not as worried about death as I am about dying.

Ecclesiastes 12:7
And the dust returns to the earth as it was, and the spirit returns to God who gave it.
2 Corinthians 5:6-8
So we are always of good courage. We know that while we are at home in the body we are away from the Lord, for we walk by faith, not by sight. Yes, we are of good courage, and we would rather be away from the body and at home with the Lord.
Psalm 23:1-6
A Psalm of David. The Lord is my shepherd; I shall not want. He makes me lie down in green pastures. He leads me beside still waters. He restores my soul. He leads me in paths of righteousness for his name's sake. Even though I walk through the valley of the shadow of death, I will fear no evil, for you are with me; your rod and your staff, they comfort me. You prepare a table before me in the presence of my enemies; you anoint my head with oil; my cup overflows. ...

OK, so maybe I shouldn't be so worried. After all, I'm not planning on going anywhere until I am 120 years old. For it is written in Genesis 6:3, And the Lord said, My spirit shall not always strive with man, for that he also is flesh: yet his days shall be an hundred and twenty years.

Day 94

Do you remember the wildly popular Wendy's commercial with the woman that would look at the hamburger of the other fast food places then look into the camera with a funny face and ask, "Where's the beef"? In effect what she was saying was, "Hey, I came here for the meat, not just a bun with condiments and a pickle!" Ever been to church and felt you only got the bun and a pickle? Or worse yet, you bit into the hamburger only to find out it was a cow pie…

2 Peter 2:1-3
But false prophets also arose among the people, just as there will be false teachers among you, who will secretly bring in destructive heresies, even denying the Master who bought them, bringing upon themselves swift destruction. And many will follow their sensuality, and because of them the way of truth will be blasphemed. And in their greed they will exploit you with false words. Their condemnation from long ago is not idle, and their destruction is not asleep.

Even pastors are entitled to a bad day here and there so cut them some slack! But, the only way to discern the Truth from the lies Peter warns about above is by studying the Bible. Occasionally you may just get the bun and the pickle at church but if you consistently get a cow pie, seek out a church that serves up a hearty portion of the Truth more often than not. Or, maybe we should just "Eat More Chikin".

Day 95

Seems a majority of people are unsatisfied with the way things are going in the world. They are hoping for a leader that will bring about change but the Bible says that's not the way it works...

Matthew 20:25-28
But Jesus called them to him and said, "You know that the rulers of the Gentiles lord it over them, and their great ones exercise authority over them. It shall not be so among you. But whoever would be great among you must be your servant, and whoever would be first among you must be your slave, even as the Son of Man came not to be served but to serve, and to give his life as a ransom for many."

It's impossible to find a servant when you are looking for a leader. We need less leaders and more servants if there is to be any change. Today let's do what Gandhi is quoted to have said and what Jesus came to do... "Be the change you wish to see in the world."

What can you do to change the world?

Day 96

Pride is a very interesting thing. I used to have a friend that went on and on about himself and how wonderful his life was and pontificated endlessly about nearly any subject to demonstrate his "wisdom". When someone tried to break in and talk, he would just talk over them with a louder voice.

Galatians 6:3
For if anyone thinks he is something, when he is nothing, he deceives himself.
Proverbs 27:2
Let another praise you, and not your own mouth; a stranger, and not your own lips.
James 4:6
But he gives more grace. Therefore it says, "God opposes the proud, but gives grace to the humble."
Proverbs 26:12
Do you see a man who is wise in his own eyes? There is more hope for a fool than for him.

Pride is like bad breath. Everyone knows you have it but you. Today let's focus on being humble. Let's do as the author Stephen Covey suggests: Seek first to understand before seeking to be understood.

Do you usually seek first to understand or to be understood?

Day 97

I recently described a friend of mine as sincere and genuinely good hearted when asked about him by a mutual friend. Wouldn't we all like to have people talking about us using the words "sincere" and "genuinely good hearted"?

Luke 8:15
As for that in the good soil, they are those who, hearing the word, hold it fast in an honest and good heart, and bear fruit with patience.
Ephesians 4:32
Be kind to one another, tenderhearted, forgiving one another, as God in Christ forgave you.
Psalm 51:10
Create in me a clean heart, O God, and renew a right spirit within me.
Matthew 5:8
"Blessed are the pure in heart, for they shall see God.
Proverbs 4:23
Keep your heart with all vigilance, for from it flow the springs of life.

When all is said and done, you will not remember the person with the beautiful face, you will remember the person with the beautiful heart. May the love of God that resides in your heart shine through your soul so that all may experience His glory through you.

Day 98

Sorry, I know this is the Second Bible Minute today, but I couldn't resist sharing this message from church this morning...

Can you believe that in church this morning we were told that there are people who actually discourage others from praying? These people believe that praying to God after a tragedy is weakness, asking God to do something to help us instead of taking it upon ourselves to avenge the wrong. I understand their frustration, but they totally miss the purpose of prayer.

Hebrews 10:22
let us draw near with a sincere heart in full assurance of faith, having our hearts sprinkled clean from an evil conscience and our bodies washed with pure water.
Psalm 73:28
But as for me, the nearness of God is my good; I have made the Lord GOD my refuge, That I may tell of all Your works.
1 Thessalonians 5:17
Pray without ceasing,

Fr. Joe Upton explained the purpose of prayer this morning this way: We are all ships on the water and God is the strong immovable dock. Prayer is the rope we throw and attach to the dock. When we pull on the rope, we are not pulling the dock closer to the boat, we are pulling the boat closer to the dock. Thus, prayer is not asking God to draw closer to us in our weakness, it is a means of drawing closer to God to give us strength.

Day 99

Have you ever been asked really tough questions about your faith? Have you even felt like you were being spiritually attacked and wished you were "one of those people that could quote chapter and verse of the Bible" to help defend your faith? As it turns out, you don't need to be "one of those people". You just need to be yourself.

1 Peter 3:15
But in your hearts honor Christ the Lord as holy, always being prepared to make a defense to anyone who asks you for a reason for the hope that is in you; yet do it with gentleness and respect,
Exodus 14:14
The Lord will fight for you, and you have only to be silent."

We are called to spread the gospel (literally translated as the Good News). You don't have to be able to quote chapter and verse to spread good news. You just need to be gentle and respectful and speak from the heart. It is often in the silence between your words that God will intervene and fight your spiritual battles for you.

What spiritual battles has God intervened in to fight on your behalf?

Day 100

My friend is a pastor at the Curtis Corner Baptist Church. He gave a great sermon that can be listened to online at his blog site that is titled "The cure for racism, bigotry, class warfare and social unrest" (http://bit.ly/2aBOeqw). He makes note of the fact that no matter who we are, when we are cut, we bleed red. He also quotes from Romans chapter 12…

"Dearly beloved, avenge not yourselves, but rather give place unto wrath: for it is written, Vengeance is mine; I will repay, saith the Lord. Therefore if thine enemy hunger, feed him; if he thirst, give him drink: for in so doing thou shalt heap coals of fire on his head. Be not overcome of evil, but overcome evil with good."

WOW! Did you get that? Be not overcome with evil, but overcome evil with good. Keep that in mind next time you listen to the nightly news or next time someone acts unjustly towards you. Overcome evil with good... Not easy but we can all do our best to follow this most difficult advice in our actions thoughts and words.

What can you do to protect yourself from evil in this world?

Day 101

When I was a kid I used to have nightmares all the time. Only very occasionally I get one these days.

Proverbs 3:24
If you lie down, you will not be afraid; when you lie down, your sleep will be sweet.
Psalm 4:8
In peace I will both lie down and sleep; for you alone, O Lord, make me dwell in safety.
Psalm 91:5
You will not fear the terror of the night, nor the arrow that flies by day,

As for me, I am confident that the reason I have less nightmares is because of how strong my faith has grown. The more I get into reading the Bible and my faith grows, the fewer nightmares I have. Maybe it's because I no longer fear the things nightmares brought because I know there is no evil and no problem God can not protect me from. There is truly power in the name of Jesus, the Son of Jehovah.

Have you called on the power in the name of Jesus recently?

Day 102

The mother of a friend of mine commented that "People are accepting what is politically correct and not morally correct." What could possibly be the consequence of that?

Exodus 20 The Ten Commandments
20 Then God spoke all these words, saying,
2 "I am the Lord your God, who brought you out of the land of Egypt, out of the house of slavery.
3 "You shall have no other gods before Me.
4 "You shall not make for yourself an idol
7 "You shall not take the name of the Lord your God in vain
8 "Remember the sabbath day, to keep it holy
12 "Honor your father and your mother
13 "You shall not murder.
14 "You shall not commit adultery.
15 "You shall not steal.
16 "You shall not bear false witness against your neighbor.
17 "You shall not covet your neighbor's house; you shall not covet your neighbor's wife…."
1 John 2:4
Whoever says "I know him" but does not keep his commandments is a liar, and the truth is not in him,
Matthew 5:19
Therefore whoever relaxes one of the least of these commandments and teaches others to do the same will be called least in the kingdom of heaven, but whoever does them and teaches them will be called great in the kingdom of heaven.

I don't know about you but I don't want to be known as a liar or be the least in the kingdom of heaven. The 10 commandments are the way to morality. I mean, check them out…they are not too hard to follow and the reward is the kingdom of heaven. Stay moral my friends.

Day 103

If you are like most people in America, you realize that the presidential primaries were a dog and pony show. It left us with two people. The problem is that now we have to choose the lesser of two evils. Is there any help from the Bible on making this important choice?

Proverbs 29:2
When the righteous increase, the people rejoice, but when the wicked rule, the people groan.
Deuteronomy 1:13
Choose for your tribes wise, understanding, and experienced men, and I will appoint them as your heads.'
Exodus 18:21
Moreover, look for able men from all the people, men who fear God, who are trustworthy and hate a bribe, and place such men over the people as chiefs of thousands, of hundreds, of fifties, and of tens.
Ecclesiastes 10:2
A wise man's heart inclines him to the right, but a fool's heart to the left.

I know, that does not exactly make the choice easier. So we are to look for a righteous person that has not done wicked things, someone who is wise, understanding and experienced and most importantly, someone that fears God. We need to choose the person who won't take a bribe from special interest groups and someone that inclines more to the right than the left. Since neither Moses nor Jesus is on the ballot, the choice is not going to be easy…

Day 104

This evening I saw the most awesome sunset I have seen in years. I literally stood there is Awe…

Psalm 65:8
They who dwell in the ends of the earth stand in awe of Your signs; You make the dawn and the sunset shout for joy.
Psalm 113:3
From the rising of the sun to its setting The name of the LORD is to be praised.

More beautiful than the most beautiful painting. More spectacular then fireworks on Independence Day in New York City. More magnificent than anything man can make. Glory to God in the highest. Thank you, God, for showing us perfection while we are still imperfect.

Day 105

Just came across an interesting word...Temperance. It is defined as the moderation or self-restraint, especially in eating and drinking. I began wondering if the Bible had any good advice on self-restraint...

Proverbs 25:16
If you have found honey, eat only enough for you, lest you have your fill of it and vomit it.
1 Peter 5:8
Be sober-minded; be watchful. Your adversary the devil prowls around like a roaring lion, seeking someone to devour.
1 Corinthians 3:16-17
Do you not know that you are God's temple and that God's Spirit dwells in you? If anyone destroys God's temple, God will destroy him. For God's temple is holy, and you are that temple.

OK, so let's re-cap. Don't eat more than your fill and stay sober. Don't do it for you, do it for God as a good steward of the temple He is letting you live in. Let's live a life with temperance avoiding excess in honor of Him.

Day 106

I once heard that you will never be remembered by what you got in this life. You will only be remembered by what you gave. It's truly a miracle, that the giving hand is never empty…

2 Corinthians 9:7
Each one must give as he has decided in his heart, not reluctantly or under compulsion, for God loves a cheerful giver.
Proverbs 11:24
One gives freely, yet grows all the richer; another withholds what he should give, and only suffers want.

True wealth is measured in what you gave away in the form of time and talents, not by how big your bank account or house is, nor is it measured by any things we amass in this life. Sometimes the most valuable things we can give away don't cost a penny like a hug, an attentive ear, our undivided attention or a sincere smile.

A smile is one thing you can give away and never need to replace. Are you giving away enough smiles, undivided attention and hugs?

Day 107

PEACE and QUIET… as I get older I seem to appreciate it more and more.

John 14:27
"Peace I leave with you, my peace I give unto you: not as the world giveth, give I unto you. Let not your heart be troubled, neither let it be afraid."

Perhaps it is why I look forward to this part of the Catholic mass:

"Priest: Lord Jesus Christ, you said to your apostles: I leave you peace, my peace I give you. Look not on our sins, but on the faith of your Church, and grant us the peace and unity of your kingdom where you live for ever and ever.

All: Amen.

Priest: The Peace of the Lord be with you always.

All: And also with your spirit.

Deacon or Priest: Let us offer each other a sign of peace.

Let us quietly offer those we encounter a sign of peace today…

Day 108

Karma…it's a "female dog"! So, I was wondering what the Bible had to say about it. Actually it's based on the religious belief in reincarnation so the Bible does not support it. However, if the concept of "what goes around, comes around" were taken a little more loosely without the reincarnation part, there are indeed a few pieces of advice from the Bible…

Galatians 6:7
Do not be deceived: God is not mocked, for whatever one sows, that will he also reap.
Luke 6:27
"But I say to you who hear, Love your enemies, do good to those who hate you,
Proverbs 26:27
Whoever digs a pit will fall into it, and a stone will come back on him who starts it rolling.

So, I guess it's a good idea to Do Onto Others… (Matthew 7:12) whether you believe in "karma" or not. According to the Bible, you don't have to wait until a "next life" to reap the rewards of being nice or suffer the consequences of being a "female dog".

What have you done recently to help someone else?

Day 109

I don't think enough people realize the importance of Gratitude. It might just be thanking the person that directs you to the bathroom in the department store, the waiter that tops off your water in the restaurant, the police officer, fireman or soldier you see in uniform during the day… or maybe just bowing your head to thank God before your meal.

Psalm 50:23
The one who offers thanksgiving as his sacrifice glorifies me; to one who orders his way rightly I will show the salvation of God!"
Luke 22:19
And he took bread, and when he had given thanks, he broke it and gave it to them, saying, "This is my body, which is given for you. Do this in remembrance of me."

Thank You. Two simple words. Try not to miss an opportunity to use them. PS- THANK YOU for taking the time to read the daily one minute Bible study.

Who will you thank today and for what?

Day 110

We all know someone that claims to know everything about everything. Whatever those around them do, they seem to have a way to do it better and a reason why your way is not good enough. Seems these people can go on for what seems like hours pontificating about the most insignificant of topics...

Romans 1:22
Claiming to be wise, they became fools,
Romans 12:16
Live in harmony with one another. Do not be haughty, but associate with the lowly. Never be wise in your own sight.
1 Timothy 1:7
Desiring to be teachers of the law, without understanding either what they are saying or the things about which they make confident assertions.

There is one thing I have learned over my lifetime, "The more you learn, the more you realize how very little you know."

What did you learn from this one?

Day 111

I had an interesting comment about my last "One Minute Bible Study". Someone proclaimed to know what the grounds for exclusion from heaven were and He was pretty sure I was going to be banished from heaven based on my modern day analogy of the story of the Good Samaritan. That got me thinking. How can someone be "un-saved" and who gets to decided that?

The bible tells us about only one unpardonable sin... Mark 3:28-29 (NASB) "Truly I say to you, all sins shall be forgiven the sons of men, and whatever blasphemies they utter; but whoever blasphemes against the Holy Spirit never has forgiveness, but is guilty of an eternal sin"—

Hebrews 6:4-6 implies that you can take yourself out of God's hands but I prefer to stand on this verse... John 10:28 I give them eternal life, and they will never perish, and no one will snatch them out of my hand.

I have always found it interesting that there are people that profess to be Christians that "Know" exactly what sins God will allow to be forgiven and which ones will definitely get you kicked out of heaven. They know exactly where the "cut-off" is to get "in" and they always seem to be just on the right side of the line themselves but they are quick to point out the people that just don't make the grade. I choose to put my faith in the Word which proclaims: Ephesians 2:8 For by grace you have been saved through faith; and that not of yourselves, it is the gift of God;

Day 112

One day a Christian was walking through a back alley and got mugged by a gang. They took his money, jewelry and even his clothes. They left him beaten and curled up on the side of the road. He was so badly beaten that his own pastor didn't recognize him and one of the people from a neighboring church passed right by him too. They even moved to the other side of the street to avoid him because they didn't want to get involved. A Muslim walked through the alley, saw him, and realized he needed help. This Muslim opened his gym bag, clothed the man and carried him to the hospital where he left money to pay for the man's care and left his name and address to bill him if the bill was more than the money he paid…

Luke 10:30-35
Jesus replied, "A man was going down from Jerusalem to Jericho, and he fell among robbers, who stripped him and beat him and departed, leaving him half dead. Now by chance a priest was going down that road, and when he saw him he passed by on the other side. So likewise a Levite, when he came to the place and saw him, passed by on the other side. But a Samaritan, as he journeyed, came to where he was, and when he saw him, he had compassion. He went to him and bound up his wounds, pouring on oil and wine. Then he set him on his own animal and brought him to an inn and took care of him. And the next day he took out two denarii and gave them to the innkeeper, saying, 'Take care of him, and whatever more you spend, I will repay you when I come back.'

There's always someone we're told to hate by the media and the government. The Russians, the Cubans, the Iranians, the _____ (you fill in the blank), and now in the media the "Mexicans" and each and every "Muslim". The point of the parables above is explained In Luke 10:36 when Jesus asks, of the three passers by, which one became a neighbor to the man that was attacked? In 10:37 the scholar answers, "The one that treated him kindly" to which Jesus said, "Go and do the same." Let's remember to be the Good Samaritan today and every day. Let's not be the one to Judge others based on what we've heard about them. Let's just be the one that treated them kindly.

Day 113

Ever reacted in Anger and regretted it? Uhhhh…. You are not alone…

Ephesians 4:26-31 (NIV)
26 "In your anger do not sin" : Do not let the sun go down while you are still angry,
27 and do not give the devil a foothold.
28 Anyone who has been stealing must steal no longer, but must work, doing something useful with their own hands, that they may have something to share with those in need.
29 Do not let any unwholesome talk come out of your mouths, but only what is helpful for building others up according to their needs, that it may benefit those who listen.
30 And do not grieve the Holy Spirit of God, with whom you were sealed for the day of redemption.
31 Get rid of all bitterness, rage and anger, brawling and slander, along with every form of malice.

Take a deep breath. Good air in, bad air out. Repeat.

What do you do to let off steam so you don't explode?

Day 114

God wants everyone to be saved and live a life of eternity with Him but many people get lost and stray away from Him. He sent his Son to gather up all His children and bring them home but look at it from God's point of view. It must be like trying to herd cats…

Luke 15:4
"What man of you, having a hundred sheep, if he has lost one of them, does not leave the ninety-nine in the open country, and go after the one that is lost, until he finds it?
2 Peter 3:9 The Message (MSG)
God isn't late with his promise as some measure lateness. He is restraining himself on account of you, holding back the End because he doesn't want anyone lost. He's giving everyone space and time to change.
John 6:39
"This is the will of Him who sent Me, that of all that He has given Me I lose nothing, but raise it up on the last day.

If there is anyone that can get the job done for God, it is Jesus. The best "cat herder" there ever was or will ever be. Yup, He will do His best to get every last one of us…

Day 115

Have you asked someone that you deeply care about if they need you to pray for them today? It's a really simple thing to do but it is powerful...

1 Timothy 2:1
First of all, then, I urge that supplications, prayers, intercessions, and thanksgivings be made for all people,

Matthew 18:19-20
Again I say to you, if two of you agree on earth about anything they ask, it will be done for them by my Father in heaven. For where two or three are gathered in my name, there am I among them."

"What can I pray for you today?" Intercessory prayer is powerful. Try it today.

How about taking the blank space below to write out some prayers, requests for God or just give thanks for what God has done, is doing or is going to do in your life?

Day 116

Ever felt like there was a valley between you and God? You need Him but there seems to be something separating you from the comfort of His embrace and the touch of His favor? Well, as it turns out, that was not God's fault, it was ours...ouch...

Isaiah 59:1-2
Behold, the Lord's hand is not shortened, that it cannot save, or his ear dull, that it cannot hear; but your iniquities have made a separation between you and your God, and your sins have hidden his face from you so that he does not hear.

Don't worry, He knew you would do that and he provided a way to get back when you got lost. The good news is that the free gift of God is eternal life with Him in Christ Jesus our Lord. Take a moment now, if you are truly ready, to sit quietly with God, ask His forgiveness for your sins, accept His Son into your heart and make Him your Lord and Savior. In those not so simple steps, you will find what you have been looking for.

Day 117

I just had a long weekend. I rested, I did things around the house that needed to be done and I spent more time with my family. Today will likely be a very busy day in the office to make up for the day I took off but I am refreshed and better prepared to be a servant again.

John 12:26
If anyone serves me, he must follow me; and where I am, there will my servant be also. If anyone serves me, the Father will honor him.

Luke 14:23
And the master said to the servant, 'Go out to the highways and hedges and compel people to come in, that my house may be filled.

Today go out and be the best servant you can possibly be. Whatever your job or career, don't just go to work; go out today to fill the needs of God's children. Serve God by serving his children to give Him honor so that His house may be filled.

Day 118

As I sit here on the eve of Independence Day, I am reminded what our forefathers fought for. They fought so that we could have FREEDOM. Turns out God talks about freedom in the Bible...

Galatians 5:1
For freedom Christ has set us free; stand firm therefore, and do not submit again to a yoke of slavery.
1 Peter 2:16
Live as people who are free, not using your freedom as a cover-up for evil, but living as servants of God.
Galatians 5:13
For you were called to freedom, brothers. Only do not use your freedom as an opportunity for the flesh, but through love serve one another.
John 8:32
And you will know the truth, and the truth will set you free."

Here's wishing you a happy, healthy and safe Fourth of July. Remember, our forefathers fought and risked their lives so that our country could enjoy the benefits of being independent and free. There is also something very freeing in being completely dependent upon God and learning the truth through His Word. That will truly set you free!

Day 119

A scientist came to God and said, "We no longer need you. With our modern technology, we can literally fix anything. We can even print fully working human organs with a 3D printer for organ transplants." God was really impressed. He asked, "How about I challenge you to a little competition?" "Sure!", said the scientist. "Let's see who can make the best human out of just plain dirt.", God suggested. The scientist said, "No problem! You're on!"

Genesis 2:7 NIV
Then the Lord God formed a man from the dust of the ground and breathed into his nostrils the breath of life, and the man became a living being.

The scientist reached down to gather a handful of dirt. "NOT SO FAST," God exclaimed, "Go get your own dirt!"

Today, really examine your heart and mind. Is there any system of organization in the universe or at least on Earth without an intelligent designer? If you can not come up with even one, why would anyone believe in evolution or the big bang theories? God created the heavens and the Earth...and ME...and you too, of course.

Day 120

It's never good to hear that friends are not getting along. It's worse when couples you know are considering a divorce. How did the love turn into discord and apathy? What advice can we possibly give them or perhaps more importantly, what can we do to avoid this in our own marriages?

Matthew 19:6
So they are no longer two but one flesh. What therefore God has joined together let not man separate."

Remember to make prayer the centerpiece of your marriage. Pray for your spouse every day and even in front of them... (Psalms 127:1) Unless the Lord builds the house, They labor in vain who build it;

Take the time to compliment your spouse in private and in public... Ephesians 4:29 Let no corrupting talk come out of your mouths, but only such as is good for building up, as fits the occasion, that it may give grace to those who hear.

Don't withhold sex from one another especially as a way to get back at one another... 1 Corinthians 7:2 But because of the temptation to sexual immorality, each man should have his own wife and each woman her own husband.

Honor your spouse and love them as Christ loves the church... (Eph 5:22-24) and (Eph 5:-25-31)

Never be afraid to say "I love you" or "I'm Sorry"... Luke 13:3 No, I tell you; but unless you repent, you will all likewise perish.

Be forgiving... Ephesians 4:32 Be kind to one another, tenderhearted, forgiving one another, as God in Christ forgave you.

Well, that was a long one but usually when that happens, it's because someone needed to hear it. I hope that if it was you, that you receive it today. If it was meant for a friend, I hope you are faithful enough to pass it along to them. May God strengthen the marriage you are in, repair the marriages that are broken and restore the broken hearts of the people whose marriages could not be saved. We pray this in the mighty name of Jesus.

Day 121

Never underestimate the power of a smile. Joy is contagious.

John 15:11
These things I have spoken to you, that my joy may be in you, and that your joy may be full.

In addition to the smile, if you share good news with someone, they are sure to share in your joy. If you smile and share The Good News with them, well, that's enough to make even Jesus smile.

BONUS for today: (since that one was so short…powerful…but short)

Is it OK to test your faith? You better believe it! A faith that can not withstand questioning and a little deep thought is a weak faith indeed…

1 John 4:1
Beloved, do not believe every spirit, but test the spirits to see whether they are from God, for many false prophets have gone out into the world.

Build up your faith by continually reading God's Word and by testing all things by it.

Day 122

We all have desires of the heart. Some desires are of the flesh, some are of the spirit. It's only human to have both but here is what the Bible says about desire…

Psalm 37:4
Delight yourself in the Lord, and he will give you the desires of your heart.

Psalm 37:5
Commit your way to the Lord; trust in him, and he will act.

Proverbs 16:1-3
The plans of the heart belong to man, but the answer of the tongue is from the Lord. All the ways of a man are pure in his own eyes, but the Lord weighs the spirit. Commit your work to the Lord, and your plans will be established.

Take great pleasure in God and reading His word, commit your work to God and trust Him to guide your steps throughout your life. If we do that, eventually what we want and what we need to grow spiritually will become the same thing.

Day 123

Everyone is so worried about being "Politically Correct" today. People are beaten down for speaking about the Truth that is found in the Bible. Even the most enthusiastic Christian, while speaking about their faith in public, lowers their voice when speaking the name of Jesus as if the mere mention of His name will offend those around them. It is as if we are living in a lion's den unable to raise our voices and speak the name of JESUS for fear of waking the hungry lions...

Daniel 6:16-23 (in part)
16 Then the king commanded, and Daniel was brought and cast into the den of lions. The king declared to Daniel, "May your God, whom you serve continually, deliver you!"... 22 My God sent his angel and shut the lions' mouths, and they have not harmed me, because I was found blameless before him; and also before you, O king, I have done no harm." 23 Then the king was exceedingly glad, and commanded that Daniel be taken up out of the den. So Daniel was taken up out of the den, and no kind of harm was found on him, because he had trusted in his God.

"This is now Jesus' world. He's the king, this is his dominion, and He gives you authority to do his work in this world. You have immense power, so live by faith. Declare into this world, speak into this world, and do into this world what Christ would do, what Christ would speak, what Christ would say. Don't be afraid. Be bold. Be bold." – Pastor Bobby Schuler

Day 124

So, what does the Bible say about other religions? Here are two verses to meditate on today about that…

1 John 4:5-8
They are from the world; therefore they speak from the world, and the world listens to them. We are from God. Whoever knows God listens to us; whoever is not from God does not listen to us. By this we know the Spirit of truth and the spirit of error. Beloved, let us love one another, for love is from God, and whoever loves has been born of God and knows God. Anyone who does not love does not know God, because God is love.

John 14:6
Jesus said to him, "I am the way, and the truth, and the life. No one comes to the Father except through me.

First and most importantly, we can know others are from God by their LOVE for one another. Secondly, the Bible is pretty clear about how to go to the Father. It is through Jesus. No matter what religion a person claims to be today, the offer is always open to accept God's Love through Jesus.

Day 125

So, what exactly does the Bible say about surfing?

Genesis 1:1 (SB by Dan Reiter)
In the beginning, God created the seas. And the Spirit of God hovered over the face of the waters. And God saw that the waters were without form, and the Lord God said, "Let there be waves," and there were waves. Then God saw that the waves were good; indeed they were very good; and so the Lord God took the rest of the day off.

Psalm 23 (SB)
The Lord is my shepherd; I shall not want. He makes me tuck down into green barrels; He leads me out through calm channels. He restores my soul; He lifts me across steep faces and engages my rail in His name.

OK, well maybe not in exactly those words, but you get the gist…

What's your hobby and how can you relate that hobby to your faith?

Day 126

Today, more than ever, we are bombarded with negativity. We must guard our hearts and our minds and shield ourselves and our families from these attacks on our spirit. Perhaps even more importantly, we must be mindful of what WE are saying to others…

Ephesians 4:29
You must let no unwholesome word come out of your mouth, but only what is beneficial for the building up of the one in need, that it may give grace to those who hear.

It's easy to get caught up in the garbage on the news, in politics, or even gossip those around us are trying to draw us into. It's tempting to join into a juicy conversation about someone else but today, choose to walk away or just speak a kind word about the person being attacked. Let's choose morality over immorality, love over apathy, kindness over intolerance, blessing over hate so that others may experience the light of God shining through us today.

How do you feel when others speak unkind words around you?

Day 127

Ever get disappointed in yourself because you knew what the right thing to do was but you chose to do another? You are certainly not alone...

Proverbs 25:28
A man without self-control is like a city broken into and left without walls.

2 Peter 1:5-7
For this very reason, make every effort to supplement your faith with virtue, and virtue with knowledge, and knowledge with self-control, and self-control with steadfastness, and steadfastness with godliness, and godliness with brotherly affection, and brotherly affection with love.

It can be as simple as choosing to eat that great looking greasy bacon, chicken ranch calzone instead of a veggie wrap. Choosing to sleep in instead of work out in the morning. Or, it can be doing something immoral instead of following God's Word. The more you read and live in God's Word, the easier it is to exhibit self-control.

What choices can you make today that will honor God?

Day 128

Faith is referenced 96 times in the old testament and 282 times in the New Testament. Some people are wired in such a way that they absolutely need to "See or Touch" something for them to believe it is real. Atheists believe that there is no God because there is not enough evidence. Thomas, one of the disciples, simply could not believe unless he had more evidence either...

John 20:27-29
27 Then He said to Thomas, "Reach here with your finger, and see My hands; and reach here your hand and put it into My side; and do not be unbelieving, but believing." 28 Thomas answered and said to Him, "My Lord and my God!" 29 Jesus said to him, "Because you have seen Me, have you believed? Blessed are they who did not see, and yet believed."

Hebrews 11:1
Now faith is the substance of things hoped for, the evidence of things not seen.

Sometimes I wish everyone had the kind of "faith" that atheists have. They have such a strong conviction and "faith" that there is no God, Heaven or Hell that they are willing to bet their very life, and life everlasting on the fact that all the rest of us are wrong.

Day 129

Boundaries are a tough thing! We need to set boundaries at work and also at play. We need to know when to say no to answering calls from work when we are with family and we need to know when to stop playing and do more good works...

Isaiah 30:15
For thus said the Lord God, the Holy One of Israel "In returning and rest you shall be saved; in quietness and in trust shall be your strength." But you were unwilling,

Mark 6:31
And he said to them, "Come away by yourselves to a desolate place and rest a while." For many were coming and going, and they had no leisure even to eat.

1 Timothy 5:8
But if anyone does not provide for his relatives, and especially for members of his household, he has denied the faith and is worse than an unbeliever.

Titus 2:7
Show yourself in all respects to be a model of good works, and in your teaching show integrity, dignity,

Turn off your cell phone and computer when you are away from work and with your family so you can be fully present with them. When you are at work, turn off your cell phone and computer and be fully present with those you serve. Rest fully, love deeply, play hard, work hard and study God's Word.

Day 130

Do you love God more than your life? If so, you have already defeated the devil…

Matthew 10:39 KJV
39 He that findeth his life shall lose it: and he that loseth his life for my sake shall find it.

Matthew 6:33 KJV
33 But seek ye first the kingdom of God, and his righteousness; and all these things shall be added unto you.

Luke 14:26 KJV
26 If any man come to me, and hate not his father, and mother, and wife, and children, and brethren, and sisters, yea, and his own life also, he cannot be my disciple.

"You are to love God so much that upon comparison any other love looks like hate. Your love for God should be beyond comparison to other people or things. When you love God more than your own life, you have taken all the leverage away from the devil. He is defeated today."- Pastor Paul Chapman (read more at Paulechapman.com)

Day 131

When bad things happen to good people, they have two choices. They can become better as a result of it or they can become bitter...

2 Corinthians 4:8-9
We are afflicted in every way, but not crushed; perplexed, but not driven to despair; persecuted, but not forsaken; struck down, but not destroyed;

James 1:12
Blessed is the man who remains steadfast under trial, for when he has stood the test he will receive the crown of life, which God has promised to those who love him.

Choose to become better.

What have you become bitter about that you can take a second look at and become "better" from instead?

Day 132

If you could turn back time and have a "do over" in your life, what would you do differently?

Proverbs 14:12-13 Amplified Bible (AMP)
12 There is a way which seems right to a man and appears straight before him,
But its end is the way of death.
13 Even in laughter the heart may be in pain,
And the end of joy may be grief.

Proverbs 14:12-13 (my interpretation)
12-13 There's a way of life that looks enticing and exciting and harmless enough;
look again—it is against the will of God and leads to eternal separation from Him.
Sure, those people that are doing whatever they please, appear to be having a good time,
but all that partying, laughter and fulfilling earthly desires will end in heartbreak.

That's a tough lesson to learn especially in this world. The truth is we can't turn back time, but going forward we can make better choices. Listen to that small voice within through prayer before you make the next decision. God is guiding your steps but it is up to you to make the decision to walk with Him.

Day 133

Are you someone that "wears your heart on your sleeve"? For those that have not heard this phrase before, it's used to describe those of us that expose our true emotions, making ourselves vulnerable by letting it all hang out.

John 11:35 Jesus wept.

It's OK to express your emotions. Anger, anxiety, awe, despair, disappointment, empathy, fear, frustration, gratitude, grief, guilt, happiness, joy, hope, loneliness, regret, remorse, sadness, shame, trust, wonder and worry. And, when your heart swells and you feel overwhelmed, it's okay for you to weep as Jesus did.

There very well may be no crying in baseball until last year, but in life, even Jesus wore His heart on his sleeve. Jesus and Wilmer Flores are real men...

Day 134

You can not save people, you can only love them.

Mark 16:15
And he said to them, "Go into all the world and proclaim the gospel to the whole creation.

1 John 4:7
Beloved, let us love one another, for love is from God, and whoever loves has been born of God and knows God.

Only God can save people through His Son, Jesus Christ. Our job is to show our love for them by sharing the Good News and being a shining example of love in our communities.

Day 135

This world is filled with chaos today. We are bombarded with information and there never seems to be a moment of silence or a moment of peace. We need to remember to take time to sit in silence with God.

Lamentations 3:26
It is good that one should wait quietly for the salvation of the Lord.

Psalm 62:5
For God alone, O my soul, wait in silence, for my hope is from him.

Proverbs 11:12
Whoever belittles his neighbor lacks sense, but a man of understanding remains silent.

We need to sit silently in prayer and just listen for God's instructions as God simultaneously sits silently during our prayer and listens to our heart's desires. Just as music is the space between the notes, prayer is the silence between the words.

Day 136

Ever feel like people "just don't get you"? Have you ever felt judged? Well we all have and we are not alone...

Luke 9:18 ESV
Now it happened that as he was praying alone, the disciples were with him. And he asked them, "Who do the crowds say that I am?"

The crowds thought he was Elijah, John the Baptist, and a host of other possibilities. Even the disciples, his closest friends, were unclear about who he was. That is except for Peter knew he was the Son of God. Jesus knew that it only mattered that God knew who he was but it must have been music to his ears to learn that Peter really "got it" and understood him and his mission here on Earth. It is truly a blessing to have someone that deeply understands you but even if you don't have a "Peter" in your life, take consolation in the fact that God created you, He loves you and really "gets you" and truly understands your mission in life.

Day 137

Ever been lied to and you Knew you were being lied to? Maybe it was a "little white lie". How did you feel about that? Maybe you told a "little white lie". More importantly how did you feel about THAT in the pit of your stomach? What could possibly be the consequence of telling a "little" lie?

2 Timothy 3:13
While evil people and impostors will go on from bad to worse, deceiving and being deceived.

Romans 6:23
For the wages of sin is death, but the free gift of God is eternal life in Christ Jesus our Lord.

Romans 3:23
For all have sinned and fall short of the glory of God,

Crud, so God says that lying is a sin whether it is a big whopper of a lie or a "little white" lie. The wages or "result" of sin is DEATH and EVERYONE has sinned. Double Crud! But hey, I have good news for you. This guy, the Son of God, Jesus Christ can wash away all your sin if you just ask for His forgiveness and allow Him into your heart. Whew, that is a relief! Thank you God.

Day 138

I once heard about three sons that tried to outdo each other in the gift they bought their Mom for her birthday. One son bought his Mom a $200K limousine with a chauffer. The second son bought his Mom a 1 million dollar mansion and the third son bought his Mom a 2 million dollar parrot that was trained for 15 years to recite the bible because the Mom was going blind and always loved reading the Bible. The mother wrote to the boys to let them know how she liked the gifts. She told the first son that she never left the house except to go to the grocery store so the limousine was really not being used. She told her second son that she was a single widow and cleaning such a big mansion was just too much trouble. But the third son, his gift was wonderful and thoughtful and the Chicken was a little scrawny but it tasted great.

Luke 21:1-4 (NKJV)
21 And He looked up and saw the rich putting their gifts into the treasury, and He saw also a certain poor widow putting in two mites. So He said, "Truly I say to you that this poor widow has put in more than all; for all these out of their abundance have put in offerings for God, but she out of her poverty put in all the livelihood that she had."

God is not impressed by how much money you have to show off or even to give away. You see, God is not even looking for us to give a financial tithe to Him out of our abundance. He is waiting for us to stop holding back and give ALL that we have, our WHOLE heart, to Him. For where your treasure is, there your heart will be also. (Matthew 6:21, Luke 12:34)

Day 139

FEAR. It is a word but it is also an acronym. It stands for False Evidence Appearing Real. There are literally hundreds of passages about fear in the Bible but here are a few to remind you about how to handle fear in our lives…

Isaiah 41:10
Fear not, for I am with you; be not dismayed, for I am your God; I will strengthen you, I will help you, I will uphold you with my righteous right hand.

1 John 4:18
There is no fear in love, but perfect love casts out fear. For fear has to do with punishment, and whoever fears has not been perfected in love.

Psalm 27:1
Of David. The Lord is my light and my salvation; whom shall I fear? The Lord is the stronghold of my life; of whom shall I be afraid?

No matter what the evidence that we are presented with, no matter how real or how scary the circumstances are, FEAR not. God is on our side, He is with us always and has protected us with His salvation and is a light unto our path even in the darkness. Whom then shall we fear?

Day 140

So, how important is it to hang out with good people? I mean, you hear all the time that Jesus hung out with "bad" people because they needed to hear the message the most. Well, the Bible has something to say about that...

1 Corinthians 15:33
Do not be deceived: "Bad company ruins good morals."

Proverbs 13:20
Whoever walks with the wise becomes wise, but the companion of fools will suffer harm.

Proverbs 6:27
Can a man carry fire next to his chest and his clothes not be burned?

1 Corinthians 5:11
But now I am writing to you not to associate with anyone who bears the name of brother if he is guilty of sexual immorality or greed, or is an idolater, reviler, drunkard, or swindler—not even to eat with such a one.

Here's the bottom line...you are not Jesus. The Bible is clear about keeping bad company and the Bible is clear about what happens when you keep good company. Love the sinners, help them when you can but don't spend most of your time keeping company with them.

Day 141

I recently put the TV on for an hour or so. Of course, there were 250 channels and nothing was on. Its uncanny how no matter what channel you flip to there is always a commercial on. One commercial was memorable for the fact that the "host" of the commercial asked the "participants" of the commercial questions and they could only answer him with emojis or emoticons. You know, the faces that represent an emotion…

Ecclesiastes 3:4
A time to weep, and a time to laugh; a time to mourn, and a time to dance;

Romans 12:15
Rejoice with those who rejoice, weep with those who weep.

Proverbs 15:13
A glad heart makes a cheerful face, but by sorrow of heart the spirit is crushed.

:'(:/ O:) ;) :) SO, just :) even when you feel like :poop:

Day 142

Isn't it cool when you see someone that is absolutely and completely in love with their job? It's magnetic in a way. They also seem to be more successful in their field. Ever wonder why?...

Proverbs 16:3
Commit your work to the Lord, and your plans will be established.

Colossians 3:23
Whatever you do, work heartily, as for the Lord and not for men,

I remember Art the door man at the Beach Club Hotel in Disney World. I never met a man so in love with his work. He would find a sincere complement for everyone that passed through the door and greet everyone with a huge smile and enthusiasm. I asked him how he could be so happy, up and excited every year we saw him, year after year. He told me, "The Lord has great plans for you, plans to prosper you and not to harm you, plans to give you hope and a future. I found the plan He had for me. Have you found yours?"

THIS IS A MUST WATCH VIDEO OF ART THE GREETER:
https://www.youtube.com/watch?v=4OpTO7V2S-U

Day 143

Ever had a moment where you couldn't remember something. Ever had that moment turn in to a lot more than one moment as you racked your brains to remember something to no avail? As you get older, it may get a little more frequent and can be scary...BUT...

John 14:26
But the Helper, the Holy Spirit, whom the Father will send in my name, he will teach you all things and bring to your remembrance all that I have said to you.

Rejoice in the knowing that through the Holy Spirit, God will remind you of all the important things you may have forgotten. You shall not forget His Word and it will comfort you all the days of your life.

When was the last time you have felt the presence of God?

Day 144

What does the Bible say about Tomorrow?

Proverbs 27:1
Do not boast about tomorrow, for you do not know what a day may bring. Truth is that we really don't know what will happen tomorrow.

James 4:13-15
Come now, you who say, "Today or tomorrow we will go into such and such a town and spend a year there and trade and make a profit"— yet you do not know what tomorrow will bring. What is your life? For you are a mist that appears for a little time and then vanishes. Instead you ought to say, "If the Lord wills, we will live and do this or that."

Instead of worrying about tomorrow, God makes this suggestion about what to do TODAY through the Psalmist: Psalm 118:24 This is the day that the Lord has made; let us rejoice and be glad in it.

Day 145

This is Memorial Day weekend and I was considering doing a Bible study about memorial. There are lots of great passages in the Bible about memorials. In fact there are 31 passages about memorials in the King James Bible and can be found at http://www.kingjamesbibleonline.org/memorial/. But then I thought about it a little more. This weekend is also (and possibly more importantly) about Sacrifice. It is about honoring the willingness of those that sacrificed their lives to protect and defend those they love and the principles they believed in. Ironically, there are 310 passages about sacrifice (exactly 10 times more)…

John 15:12-14
"This is my commandment, that you love one another as I have loved you. Greater love has no one than this, that someone lay down his life for his friends. You are my friends if you do what I command you.

Ephesians 5:2
And walk in love, as Christ also hath loved us, and hath given himself for us an offering and a sacrifice to God for a sweet smelling savour.

Hebrews 10:12
But this man, after he had offered one sacrifice for sins for ever, sat down on the right hand of God;

Hebrews 11:4
By faith Abel offered unto God a more excellent sacrifice than Cain, by which he obtained witness that he was righteous, God testifying of his gifts: and by it he being dead yet speaketh.

Yes, I know, that is a lot for a one minute Bible study but this is a heavy subject. "Greater love has no one than this, that someone lay down his life for his friends." That is a BIG thought! And all those that sacrificed their lives for our freedom, when we remember them this weekend…by it they being dead, they yet speaketh.

Day 146

Odds are you have been sick (or dis-eased as we Chiropractors call it) before and chances are you'll be sick or dis-eased again before you leave this earthly body. Fear not, the Power that created your body IS the Power that heals the body…

Isaiah 41:10
Fear not, for I am with you; be not dismayed, for I am your God; I will strengthen you, I will help you, I will uphold you with my righteous right hand.

Jeremiah 17:14
Heal me, O Lord, and I shall be healed; save me, and I shall be saved, for you are my praise.

Jeremiah 33:6
Behold, I will bring to it health and healing, and I will heal them and reveal to them abundance of prosperity and security.

Not only will God heal you, but He will strengthen you, uphold you, and provide you with abundance, prosperity and security. All of a sudden I'm not so worried about being sick OR dis-eased.

Have you seen evidence of God's healing power in your life?

Day 147

Ever wonder if you did "All You Could Do?" and if "You Did Enough"?...

Revelation 20:11-15 ESV
Then I saw a great white throne and him who was seated on it. From his presence earth and sky fled away, and no place was found for them. And I saw the dead, great and small, standing before the throne, and books were opened. Then another book was opened, which is the book of life. And the dead were judged by what was written in the books, according to what they had done. And the sea gave up the dead who were in it, Death and Hades gave up the dead who were in them, and they were judged, each one of them, according to what they had done. Then Death and Hades were thrown into the lake of fire. This is the second death, the lake of fire. And if anyone's name was not found written in the book of life, he was thrown into the lake of fire.

All you can do is all you can do, but ALL you can do is enough. Our name is written in the Book of Life not just because of what we do but because of our faith in Jesus.

Day 148

Ever heard the phrase, "God will never give you more than you can handle"? Biblically, it is sort of a Lie. It only applies to temptation in 1 Corinthians 10:13. Even Jesus cried out when he was given more than He could handle and the Psalmist shares our frustrations and resentment as well…

Matthew 26:38 and 39 (NASB)
Then He said to them, "My soul is deeply grieved, to the point of death…"
"My Father, if it is possible, let this cup pass from Me; yet not as I will, but as You will."

Psalm 22:1-2
My God, my God, why have You forsaken me? Far from my deliverance are the words of my groaning. O my God, I cry by day, but You do not answer; And by night, but I have no rest.

Hey, it's OK to admit that you have more on your plate than you can handle right now. In that acknowledgment we are in effect saying, "God, I really need you right now." It is in our suffering that we find we are not alone. In fact, it is God who is sits beside us in the person of Jesus suffering with us. And when it is time, His promise to us is that He will stand up first, reach over and extend His hand to help you up. He will then dry your eyes and lead you out of the darkness and into the light. He will take your rough path and make it smooth again. Yes, that is a promise…Isaiah 25:8, 42:16

Day 149

Do you know what a zealot is? It is a person that s fanatical and uncompromising in pursuit of their religious, political, or other ideals. These 'fanatics' will often go to extreme measures to see that everyone follows their beliefs. So, is that a good thing? I mean, what measures would you go to in order to have someone accept Jesus as their Savior? What would you do to save someone from eternal separation from God?

Romans 10:2 ESV
For I bear them witness that they have a zeal for God, but not according to knowledge.

Isaiah 59:17
He put on righteousness as a breastplate, and a helmet of salvation on his head; he put on garments of vengeance for clothing, and wrapped himself in zeal as a cloak.

John 2:17
His disciples remembered that it was written, "Zeal for your house will consume me."

Today we live in an age of "terror" where some Muslims have become zealots. They go to extreme measures including violence and murder to achieve their goals. The difference between the terrorists and us is that even though we are zealots for Christ, we have been commissioned by God to zealously spread the gospel WITHOUT breaking any of the commandments.

Day 150

Here is an interesting Biblical principle: Whatever you want more of, give more of it away…

Luke 6:38
Give, and it will be given to you. Good measure, pressed down, shaken together, running over, will be put into your lap. For with the measure you use it will be measured back to you."

Are you giving to others in a way that is pleasing to the Lord? What are you holding onto in your life that you should be giving away? Take a minute or two to write some of those things down below:

Day 151

Culture (cult-ure) is based upon some form of religious or spiritual worldview. When the traditional beliefs of a nation erode, the nation dies. Religion provides the set of standards that govern a nation. Historian Will Durant said, "There is no significant example in history, before our time, of a society successfully maintaining moral life without the aid of religion."

Romans 13:8-10 (how fitting...think...fall of the Roman Empire)
Owe no one anything, except to love each other, for the one who loves another has fulfilled the law. For the commandments, "You shall not commit adultery, You shall not murder, You shall not steal, You shall not covet," and any other commandment, are summed up in this word: "You shall love your neighbor as yourself." Love does no wrong to a neighbor; therefore love is the fulfilling of the law.

Unfortunately, the USA has embarked on a journey to maintain a society without a religious code. The Ten Commandments are removed from the walls, and religious values are torn from the public places. Christian principles are no longer taught in the public schools and the notion that God Created the world is often ridiculed in education and media. One has to wonder what the fate of this country will be in the future. And still, we are called to Love One Another...

Day 152

When your WHY is strong enough, you will figure out HOW to accomplish your goals…

Hebrews 12:2
"Looking unto Jesus the author and finisher of our faith; who for the joy that was set before him endured the cross, despising the shame, and is set down at the right hand of the throne of God."

Jesus went willingly to the cross for The JOY of PLEASING His Father. "For this reason the Father loves me, because I lay down my life that I may take it up again" John 10:17. That was a BIG WHY. What would you do to please your Father in Heaven?

Here is a video that exemplifies the Bible principle above:
https://www.facebook.com/thediscussion15/videos/494134840796583/

Day 153

Read a quote a friend posted: "We are all receiving Charity. There is something in each of us that cannot be naturally loved." C. S. Lewis

Romans 5:8
But God shows his love for us in that while we were still sinners, Christ died for us.

Agape love...that is very powerful. As the late Dr. Robert H. Schuler would say... And all God's people said, "WOW!!!"

How can we show God's Agape love today? Write down a few ideas below:

Day 154

This morning I just wanted you to know that you are AWESOME, SPECIAL, WONDERFUL and UNIQUE! Listen, that's not just my opinion, God thinks so too...

Jeremiah 1:5
"Before I formed you in the womb I knew you, and before you were born I consecrated you; I appointed you a prophet to the nations."

Psalm 139:14
I praise you, for I am fearfully and wonderfully made. Wonderful are your works; my soul knows it very well.

Genesis 1:27
So God created man in his own image, in the image of God he created him; male and female he created them.

Ephesians 2:10
For we are his workmanship, created in Christ Jesus for good works, which God prepared beforehand, that we should walk in them.

Matthew 10:30
But even the hairs of your head are all numbered.

Go out there today and let someone else know that they are Awesome, Special, Wonderful and Unique. When they ask you how you know that, tell 'em God said so through His Word.

Day 155

Our minds and bodies are constantly creating new things. Ever read a book that was really good or watched a movie and no sooner than you read the last page or left the movie theater, you were looking forward to the sequel? God kinda feels the same way about every person on Earth after they are born in to this world...

Isaiah 43:18-19
"Remember not the former things, nor consider the things of old. Behold, I am doing a new thing; now it springs forth, do you not perceive it? I will make a way in the wilderness and rivers in the desert.

2 Corinthians 5:17
Therefore, if anyone is in Christ, he is a new creation. The old has passed away; behold, the new has come.

When we accept Jesus as our Lord and Savior and let him into our heart, we literally become a new creation... a sequel to the original born here on Earth...except better, WAY better than the original!

Day 156

I have known many people that pride themselves on being a perfectionist. There are a few problems with this…the pride part and the illusion that we can be perfect…

1 John 1:8
If we say we have no sin, we deceive ourselves, and the truth is not in us.

Ecclesiastes 7:20
Surely there is not a righteous man on earth who does good and never sins.

Proverbs 11:2
When pride comes, then comes disgrace, but with the humble is wisdom.

Proverbs 29:23
One's pride will bring him low, but he who is lowly in spirit will obtain honor.

I suppose the other problem with the fact that people pride themselves on being a perfectionist is that I do that. Lord forgive me for my arrogance and know that I am grateful that your grace is sufficient and that your power is made perfect in my weakness.

Day 157

Sunny days are awesome. Everything seems better on a sunny day. They seem to hide all the problems in our life. Rain is an even more awesome thing. For when it rains and the roof leaks, it points out all the spots in the roof that are imperfect and impure. It points out the damage to the roof that would have gone unnoticed and gotten worse had it not rained...

Psalm 31:12
I have been forgotten like one who is dead; I have become like a broken vessel.

1 Peter 5:10
And after you have suffered a little while, the God of all grace, who has called you to his eternal glory in Christ, will himself restore, confirm, strengthen, and establish you.

We ALL break and are imperfect like the roof. We blow our imperfection off and think its no big deal and that no one will notice...including God. But, we're wrong. What's crazier is that all we need to do to be "fixed" is to admit our imperfection to God and ask for forgiveness and then go and sin no more. Don't wait until it is too late...Don't wait until it rains before you fix "your roof".

Day 158

Patience is certainly a virtue. One that I do not possess! When I want something done, I want it done NOW. I guess you can say I'm not a good team player. Many hands makes light work but if those hands are not ready and willing RIGHT NOW, my pride tells me I can do it NOW, by myself, and get it done even better. THAT is NOT very biblical...

Habakkuk 2:3
For still the vision awaits its appointed time; it hastens to the end—it will not lie. If it seems slow, wait for it; it will surely come; it will not delay.

Lamentations 3:25
The Lord is good to those who wait for him, to the soul who seeks him.

Psalm 27:14
Wait for the Lord; be strong, and let your heart take courage; wait for the Lord!

Waiting is not easy. It takes strength, courage and often it requires great faith. Every vision was given to us by God Himself and has an appointed time. Take a deep breath, trust in The Lord and just Wait.

Day 159

What does the Bible say about integrity?

Proverbs 10:9
Whoever walks in integrity walks securely, but he who makes his ways crooked will be found out.

Proverbs 28:6
Better is a poor man who walks in his integrity than a rich man who is crooked in his ways.

in·teg·ri·ty
inˈtegrədē/
noun
1.the quality of being honest and having strong moral principles; moral uprightness.
"he is known to be a man of integrity"
synonyms: honesty, probity, rectitude, honor, good character, principle(s), ethics, morals, righteousness, morality, virtue, decency, fairness, scrupulousness, sincerity, truthfulness, trustworthiness
"I never doubted his integrity"
2. the state of being whole and undivided.

Day 160

NO JOY? Fake it till you make it.

Romans 15:13
May the God of hope fill you with all joy and peace in believing, so that by the power of the Holy Spirit you may abound in hope.

Philippians 4:4
Rejoice in the Lord always; again I will say, Rejoice.

You're not alone, sometimes its hard to put on a smile....just do it anyway. Smiles are contagious. Start with a smile then look in the mirror.

Sometimes we forget to be nice to the person in the mirror. Write one or two things you will do today to be nice to yourself today.

Day 161

Lyrics of "If We're Honest" by FRANCESCA BATTISTELLI:
Truth is harder than a lie
The dark seems safer than the light
And everyone has a heart that loves to hide
I'm a mess and so are you
We've built walls nobody can get through
Yeah, it may be hard, but the best thing we could ever do, ever do

Psalm 34:18
The Lord is near to the brokenhearted and saves the crushed in spirit.

Psalm 51:17
The sacrifices of God are a broken spirit; a broken and contrite heart, O God, you will not despise.

Psalm 147:3
He heals the brokenhearted and binds up their wounds.

Bring your brokenness, and I'll bring mine
'Cause love can heal what hurt divides
And mercy's waiting on the other side
If we're honest
If we're honest

Day 162

This world is filled with many people that wish to be leaders.

1 Timothy 4:12
Let no one despise you for your youth, but set the believers an example in speech, in conduct, in love, in faith, in purity.

Truth is though, that we need less leaders and more servants.

AND

Did you know that you have TWO bodies? Being healthy requires keeping both of them fed.

1 Corinthians 15:44
It is sown a natural body; it is raised a spiritual body. If there is a natural body, there is also a spiritual body.

We all know that you are what you eat. We are aware that there are GMO foods and Non-GMO and Non-GMO is better. There are organic foods and non-organic foods and organic foods are better. What are you feeding your spiritual body?

Day 163

Well, it's almost Mother's day. I suppose we should pause for a moment and see what the Bible has to say about mothers…

Proverbs 31:25-30
Strength and dignity are her clothing, and she laughs at the time to come. She opens her mouth with wisdom, and the teaching of kindness is on her tongue. She looks well to the ways of her household and does not eat the bread of idleness. Her children rise up and call her blessed; her husband also, and he praises her: "Many women have done excellently, but you surpass them all."…

Strength, dignity, a good sense of humor to put up with us, wisdom, kindness, always working for us, never idle, blessed… Yup that is a good start to a list that would describe the women in our lives that are mothers.

Day 164

The Bible teaches about important things which, when read for the first time, seem almost insignificant but everything is in the Word for a reason. Maybe you can relate to this analogy that Paul discusses with all who would read his writing for centuries to come...

2 Corinthians 12:7-10 (NASB)
A Thorn in the Flesh
7 Because of the surpassing greatness of the revelations, for this reason, to keep me from exalting myself, there was given me a thorn in the flesh, a messenger of Satan to torment me—to keep me from exalting myself! 8 Concerning this I implored the Lord three times that it might leave me. 9 And He has said to me, "My grace is sufficient for you, for power is perfected in weakness." Most gladly, therefore, I will rather boast about my weaknesses, so that the power of Christ may dwell in me. 10 Therefore I am well content with weaknesses, with insults, with distresses, with persecutions, with difficulties, for Christ's sake; for when I am weak, then I am strong.

Have you thanked God for the thorns in your side today? It is in our weakness that we are made strong.

Day 165

Are you considering making a change in your business, your personal life, your spiritual life or just considering how to advise a friend on how to make a decision that will change the course of their lives?

Isaiah 43:19
See, I am doing a new thing! Now it springs up; do you not perceive it? I am making a way in the wilderness and streams in the wasteland.

Philippians 4:6-7
Do not be anxious about anything, but in everything by prayer and supplication with thanksgiving let your requests be made known to God. And the peace of God, which surpasses all understanding, will guard your hearts and your minds in Christ Jesus.

Ecclesiastes 3:1
For everything there is a season, and a time for every matter under heaven:

If you are feeling an idea spring up inside you, make sure it is congruent with your belief system. Once you have really prayed about it, then don't be afraid to follow through and make that change. Seasons change. Embrace the new one when it arrives.

Day 166

We are confronted with many decisions in life. Some are trivial, some are important and some will profoundly change our lives forever going forward. When we stand at any fork in the road of life, how should we make our decision which way to go?

James 1:5
If any of you lacks wisdom, let him ask God, who gives generously to all without reproach, and it will be given him.

Isaiah 30:21
And your ears shall hear a word behind you, saying, "This is the way, walk in it," when you turn to the right or when you turn to the left.

That is VERY cool. That means that when we are in the Word, all the wisdom that Solomon asked for is available to us and that small voice we hear and recognize as "intuition" or a "gut feeling" may indeed be Him guiding our steps.

Day 167

I was at a conference yesterday and heard many good speakers. Some were good, some were great but one just stood out above the others. It was not the loudest of them. It was not the most well known of them. It was one whose voice stood out among the others because of his obedience to God. Right away I knew what he was saying came through him, not from him...

Proverbs 1:1-33
The proverbs of Solomon, son of David, king of Israel: To know wisdom and instruction, to understand words of insight, to receive instruction in wise dealing, in righteousness, justice, and equity; to give prudence to the simple, knowledge and discretion to the youth— Let the wise hear and increase in learning, and the one who understands obtain guidance, ...

Matthew 7:24-25
"Everyone then who hears these words of mine and does them will be like a wise man who built his house on the rock. And the rain fell, and the floods came, and the winds blew and beat on that house, but it did not fall, because it had been founded on the rock.

Because this person is also a friend, I know he had sought wisdom and instruction from other wise people and that he had taken time to sit quietly in prayer to seek guidance, insight and instruction from God. When we choose the people we spend most of our time with, it's a good idea to seek those that have built their house on a Rock. Yesterday I most certainly increased in learning from what came THROUGH him, from Him by the Grace of God. Don't fill your world with the popular people that scream the loudest, fill your world with the people that pray the longest.

Day 168

I understand that we need to extend an olive branch to those that have offended us but when is enough enough?

Mark 11:25 ESV
And whenever you stand praying, forgive, if you have anything against anyone, so that your Father also who is in heaven may forgive you your trespasses.

Matthew 18:21-22 ESV
Then Peter came up and said to him, "Lord, how often will my brother sin against me, and I forgive him? As many as seven times?" Jesus said to him, "I do not say to you seven times, but seventy times seven

Crud! That's not the answer I was hoping for...but there it is.

Who have you been holding a grudge against? Who have you failed to forgive? Make a commitment to write their names down here and forgive them in person, over the phone, or through prayer or a letter if they are no longer alive.

Day 169

WOW, everyone was so worried today that the country is going to go to H-E-double hockey sticks with the election of any of the front runners for president. CALM DOWN FOLKS!!!...

Psalm 47:8
God reigns over the nations; God is seated on his holy throne.

Romans 8:28
And we know that all things work together for good to them that love God, to them who are the called according to his purpose.

Guess who will be sitting on the throne the day after the elections? Yup, you got it, GOD will be sitting on the throne and in charge. Know that He can take anything bad and make good out of it!

Day 170

It was primary election day yesterday. There are so many important lessons to be learned from elections. Choosing wisely, the importance of praying for guidance, being leery of deception by empty promises, the desire to be represented instead of ruled over and …

Deuteronomy 1:13 ESV
Choose for your tribes wise, understanding, and experienced men, and I will appoint them as your heads.'

1 Timothy 2:1-2 ESV
First of all, then, I urge that supplications, prayers, intercessions, and thanksgivings be made for all people, for kings and all who are in high positions, that we may lead a peaceful and quiet life, godly and dignified in every way.

Ephesians 5:6 ESV
Let no one deceive you with empty words, for because of these things the wrath of God comes upon the sons of disobedience.

Judges 8:23 ESV
Gideon said to them, "I will not rule over you, and my son will not rule over you; the Lord will rule over you."

Acts 5:29 ESV
But Peter and the apostles answered, "We must obey God rather than men.

Perhaps the most important lesson to be learned… No matter who is elected, our trust and faith can only be in God, and in God alone.

Day 171

Ever notice that it's tougher to wake up in the morning after working long and hard the day before? It's even tougher when the sound of the rain hitting the roof. It's almost hypnotic. I always feel more tired on those mornings and wish that I could just stay under my nice warm covers just a "few more minutes" to get more rest...

Matthew 11:28-30 ESV
Come to me, all who labor and are heavy laden, and I will give you rest. Take my yoke upon you, and learn from me, for I am gentle and lowly in heart, and you will find rest for your souls. For my yoke is easy, and my burden is light."

Isaiah 40:31 ESV
But they who wait for the Lord shall renew their strength; they shall mount up with wings like eagles; they shall run and not be weary; they shall walk and not faint.

Then miraculously, once out of bed, I remember how lucky I am to have a job. I'm lucky to have an opportunity to go out and make a difference in this world by making a difference in my office today. Work is fun, I love to work. Don't get me wrong...I love to sleep, but more so I love to work.

Day 172

I once heard that it takes more muscles to frown than it does to smile…I must be lazy…

Proverbs 15:13-14 ESV
A glad heart makes a cheerful face, but by sorrow of heart the spirit is crushed. The heart of him who has understanding seeks knowledge, but the mouths of fools feed on folly.

Psalm 34:5 ESV
Those who look to him are radiant, and their faces shall never be ashamed.

Numbers 6:25 ESV
The Lord make his face to shine upon you and be gracious to you;

…OR MAYBE…I am just so very grateful for the grace that God gave me through the sacrifice of my Lord and Savior Jesus Christ…

Day 173

I had an interesting conversation with my beautiful, intelligent and compassionate daughter about the welfare system. I expressed my dislike of the fact that in America 35% of the people are on welfare that 51% of the people working are paying to support them. (The other 14% are over 65 and collecting the money that they paid in with their own hard work.) My daughter asked if I thought that we should just stop paying the "welfare families". I suggested that we have them do community and infrastructure work for that money and if they chose not to work, it would be like in the real world, you would not get paid. She asked what I would do if they decided to still not work…should we not feed them or give them shelter? What would Jesus have us do?

Deuteronomy 15:7
"If there is a poor man with you, one of your brothers, in any of your towns in your land which the LORD your God is giving you, you shall not harden your heart, nor close your hand from your poor brother;
John 13:34-35
"A new command I give you: Love one another. As I have loved you, so you must love one another. 35 By this everyone will know that you are my disciples, if you love one another."
1 John 3:17
If anyone has material possessions and sees a brother or sister in need but has no pity on them, how can the love of God be in that person?
Proverbs 19:17
Whoever is kind to the poor lends to the LORD, and he will reward them for what they have done.
Isaiah 58:10
and if you spend yourselves in behalf of the hungry and satisfy the needs of the oppressed, then your light will rise in the darkness, and your night will become like the noonday.

CONVICTED!! It's easy to pass judgment, be bitter and sour about high taxes, having to work hard for a living and have animosity towards the people "living off the system" but God in the Old Testament and Jesus in the New Testament admonish us to give out of our own abundance that He provided for us. We should be grateful that we have the means to give to the poor and remember that the giving hand is NEVER empty.

Day 174

Tonight we had a great night of fellowship with some friends of ours and we are looking forward to many other nights with them and with other couples that we know. Often I make excuses why we have no time to get together but in the end, it is always good to spend time with like minded friends that have similar values…

1 John 1:7 ESV
But if we walk in the light, as he is in the light, we have fellowship with one another, and the blood of Jesus his Son cleanses us from all sin
1 Thessalonians 5:11
Therefore encourage one another and build one another up, just as you are doing.
Hebrews 10:25
Not neglecting to meet together, as is the habit of some, but encouraging one another, and all the more as you see the Day drawing near.
Ecclesiastes 4:9-12
Two are better than one, because they have a good reward for their toil. For if they fall, one will lift up his fellow. But woe to him who is alone when he falls and has not another to lift him up! Again, if two lie together, they keep warm, but how can one keep warm alone? And though a man might prevail against one who is alone, two will withstand him—a threefold cord is not quickly broken.
Hebrews 10:24
And let us consider how to stir up one another to love and good works,
Proverbs 27:17
Iron sharpens iron, and one man sharpens another.

WOW, there are a lot of good, Biblical reasons to hang out with your friends more…

Day 175

Praying for one another is so very important. A friend once told me that he appreciated when someone told him that they were "thinking of him in his time of need" but what he really 'needed' was their prayer. Often it's tough to find the words to pray for one another. Don't worry, the Holy Spirit has you covered...

Romans 8:26-27 ESV
Likewise the Spirit helps us in our weakness. For we do not know what to pray for as we ought, but the Spirit himself intercedes for us with groanings too deep for words. And he who searches hearts knows what is the mind of the Spirit, because the Spirit intercedes for the saints according to the will of God.

So, just stand or sit quietly, perhaps it feels right to fold your hands, maybe even fall to your knees and let God hear the yearnings of your heart for those you care about as you intercede on their behalf. And since you are already talking to God, "confess your sins and pray for one another, that you may be healed. The prayer of a righteous person has great power as it is working." (loosely from James 5:16)

Day 176

In my Chiropractic office, after I adjust my patients, I remind them that they are once again a bright light and admonish them to go SHINE in our community. An adjustment re-connects the brain to the body by removing interference caused by subluxations and allows a clear communication between the brain and all 70 trillion tissue cells. On a deeper level, an adjustment re-connects man the spiritual with man the physical thereby making them a whole human being again so that the light of God can SHINE through them…

Matthew 5:14-16 (NASB)
14 "You are the light of the world. A city set on a hill cannot be hidden; 15 nor does anyone light a lamp and put it under a basket, but on the lamp stand, and it gives light to all who are in the house. 16 Let your light shine before men in such a way that they may see your good works, and glorify your Father who is in heaven.

One of my favorite songs is by the Newsboys and is called SHINE. The song admonishes us to "SHINE, Make 'em wonder whatcha got, make 'em wish that they were not on the outside looking bored. SHINE, Let it shine before all men, let them see good works and then let 'em glorify the Lord."

Day 177

"The Christian shoemaker does his duty not by putting little crosses on the shoes, but by making good shoes, because God is interested in good craftsmanship."
— Martin Luther

1 Peter 4:10-11 ESV
As each has received a gift, use it to serve one another, as good stewards of God's varied grace: whoever speaks, as one who speaks oracles of God; whoever serves, as one who serves by the strength that God supplies—in order that in everything God may be glorified through Jesus Christ. To him belong glory and dominion forever and ever. Amen.

Romans 12:6-8 ESV
Having gifts that differ according to the grace given to us, let us use them: if prophecy, in proportion to our faith; if service, in our serving; the one who teaches, in his teaching; the one who exhorts, in his exhortation; the one who contributes, in generosity; the one who leads, with zeal; the one who does acts of mercy, with cheerfulness.

I'm not interested in converting every person that walks into my Chiropractic office. I'm interested in giving every person a principled, specific, scientific, Chiropractic Adjustment with love and caring in such a way that honors God for entrusting me with this responsibility. Whatever it is that you do, do it with honesty and integrity so that those you serve will see the light of Christ shining through you.

Day 178

I just observed an interesting and sad thing...a Facebook fight. It must have started with angry words that were exchanged by personal messages and escalated into one person over-reacting by giving a "poor rating" on the other's business page. It became even nastier as the argument was made public in a group they both belong to and I had the misfortune of seeing...

Ecclesiastes 7:20-22 (NASB)
20 Indeed, there is not a righteous man on earth who continually does good and who never sins. 21 Also, do not take seriously all words which are spoken, so that you will not hear your servant cursing you. 22 For you also have realized that you likewise have many times cursed others.

Facebook and social media are a double edged sword. I could never share the Gospel on this page or my advice to Chiroprac-TORs on my Chiropractic Cash Only Practice page without Facebook but it comes at a price. We have become absorbed with this media which is without facial expression, empathy, voice inflection or consequential immediate feedback for the things we say. In this world of online communication, a misplaced 'comma' can change meaning and become a sword that strikes a fatal blow. It is true, now more than ever, that "The pen is mightier than the sword".

Day 179

Although my Grandpa was a loving soul, he often advised me against talking about religion and politics with friends (if I wanted to keep them as friends). Grandpa felt that it was the laws of religion and the doctrine the accompanied it which caused the tension and we should instead focus on worshiping God Himself. In essence, religious doctrine may separate us but God's love unites us.

"You must love the Lord your God with all your heart, all your soul, and all your mind. This is the first and greatest commandment. A second is equally important: 'Love your neighbor as yourself. The entire law and all the demands of the prophets are based on these two commandments." ~ Matt 22:37-40

Interestingly, this also seems to be the message of Pope Francis in his newly published document entitled "The Joy of Love". In that document, he warns about trying to find salvation in the law rather than in God. Fr. Jared summarized it best in Christ The King's Parish newsletter when he wrote, "Francis is fighting the same battle that Jesus fought: a battle against those who worship religion instead of worshipping God."

Day 180

Ever been really frustrated with someone or by something someone else has said about you, a family member or friend?

Proverbs 29:11 ESV

A fool gives full vent to his spirit, but a wise man quietly holds it back.

Exodus 14:14 ESV
The Lord will fight for you, and you have only to be silent."

In other words, don't get mad…let God get you even.

Have you been mad about something or at someone? Can you make a commitment to let it go and let God take care of it today?

Day 181

The Old Testament has a lot of laws to follow and sins to avoid. Some sins were considered an abomination and ALL sins lead to death. Not just any death, but Eternal Death, a separation from our Creator forever. This leads many Christians to feel compelled to judge others, often out of love, and attack them verbally, often out of concern. I'm concerned they may not fully understand the New Testament…

John 8:7 (KJV)
7 So when they continued asking him, he lifted up himself, and said unto them, He that is without sin among you, let him first cast a stone at her.

Matthew 7:1-3 (KJV)
Judge not, that ye be not judged.
2 For with what judgment ye judge, ye shall be judged: and with what measure ye mete, it shall be measured to you again.
3 And why beholdest thou the mote that is in thy brother's eye, but considerest not the beam that is in thine own eye?

Don't ignore the Old Testament, it is still the same loving God there trying to keep the body of Christ pure and clean though it may not appear that way on the surface but remember that one sin is not better or worse than another. Sin is Sin. We are saved through grace. Let's be shining examples of Love, Agape Love without hate or judgment. I believe that and that alone will attract others to Christ and save them from whatever sin they need to be saved from as we are saved from all our own sins in the process.

Day 182

Ever been accused of having an ulterior motive for consistently reaching out and doing acts of kindness. My friend told me that no one is that nice....ouch.

John 13:34-35
A new commandment I give to you, that you love one another: just as I have loved you, you also are to love one another. By this all people will know that you are my disciples, if you have love for one another."

Ephesians 4:32
Be kind to one another, tenderhearted, forgiving one another, as God in Christ forgave you.

Luke 6:31 ESV
And as you wish that others would do to you, do so to them.

So, I get it... We are in this world but not of it. When Christ is in you, it is easy to see that going out of our way to do things for strangers is what we are called to do as Christians. But, to those that are still in the dark, Godless and Of This World, our kindness and tithing of our time, talents and treasures will always seem to have an ulterior motive. Be The Light.

PS- Hebrews 13:1-2 Let brotherly love continue. Do not neglect to show hospitality to strangers, for thereby some have entertained angels unawares.

Who knows, maybe unbeknownst to us, the next person we will be kind to will be an angel or even Jesus Himself and by doing so, we will store up treasure in heaven. Even Jesus taught us, "Verily I say unto you, Since you have done it unto one of the least of these my brethren, you have done it unto me."

Day 183

What does the Bible say about working hard?

Proverbs 6:6-11
6 Go to the ant, O sluggard;
consider her ways, and be wise.
7 Without having any chief,
officer, or ruler,
8 she prepares her bread in summer
and gathers her food in harvest.
9 How long will you lie there, O sluggard?
When will you arise from your sleep?
10 A little sleep, a little slumber,
a little folding of the hands to rest,
11 and poverty will come upon you like a robber,
and want like an armed man.

This advice from the Bible is what we old folks call a Strong Work Ethic.

How is your work ethic?

Day 184

I am sitting here drinking the first of 3 non-dairy green smoothies that I will have to sustain my body today until I get home tonight. I actually like them. Today I made it in the Vitamixer with spinach, banana, strawberry, pineapple and mango with a touch of lemon in about 4 cups of water. Is there any point to eating healthy?

1 Corinthians 3:16-17
Do you not know that you are God's temple and that God's Spirit dwells in you? If anyone destroys God's temple, God will destroy him. For God's temple is holy, and you are that temple.

1 Corinthians 10:31
So, whether you eat or drink, or whatever you do, do all to the glory of God.

If my body really is the temple of God, I think it is a good idea to keep the temple as fit as possible and maintain it and preserve it to the best of my abilities. Maintaining it includes sleeping 6-8 hours a day, reading the Bible and being positive, exercising, having the brain fully connected to the 70 trillion cells in the body without interference (be adjusted weekly), and yes, eat healthy foods comprised mostly of veggies and fruit.

Day 185

Here is a different kind of Bible study for today:
You don't have to actually answer the questions. Just ponder, read straight through, and you'll get the point...
1. Name the five wealthiest people in the world.
2. Name the last four Heisman trophy winners.
3. Name the last three winners of the Miss America pageant.
4. Name three people who have won the Nobel or Pulitzer Prize.
5. Name the last four Academy Award winners for best actor and actress.
6. Name the last three World Series winners.
7. Name the last three Super Bowl winners.

How did you do? The point is, none of us remember the headliners of yesterday. These are no second-rate achievers. They are the best in their fields. But the applause dies .. Awards tarnish ... Achievements are forgotten. Accolades and certificates are buried with their owners.

Matthew 6:19 - "Do not lay up for yourselves treasures on earth, where moth and rust destroy and where thieves break in and steal,

Here's another quiz. See how you do on this one:
1. List two teachers who aided your journey through school.
2. Name three friends who have helped you through a difficult time.
3. Name four people who have taught you something worthwhile.
4. Name 3 people who have made you feel appreciated and special.
5. Think of five people you enjoy spending time with.

Easier?

The lesson: The people who make a difference in your life are not the ones with the most credentials, the most money ... or the most awards.
They simply are the ones who care the most.

Philippians 2:4- do not merely look out for your own personal interests, but also for the interests of others.

Galatians 6:2- Bear one another's burdens, and thereby fulfill the law of Christ.

Romans 12:10 -Be devoted to one another in brotherly love; give preference to one another in honor;

Day 186

Yesterday in Boston I made a left when clearly the sign said no left turn...and I got pulled over by the state police waiting down the road. Ever done something wrong even when you knew better but thought you had a good excuse?

James 4:17
So whoever knows the right thing to do and fails to do it, for him it is sin.

I told the officer I was sorry and I knew I was wrong. I was let go with a written warning...he showed mercy on me. Tell God you are sorry and He will show you His mercy.

Have you confessed your sins to God recently? How about doing that right now? ...He's waiting to forgive you if you give Him a chance.

Day 187

So, I was in church tonight and I had the pleasure of sitting just in front of two little children who were not interested in being in church. Despite the grandparents trying to calm them down, they were playing and yelling behind me and I missed the homily. I looked back at them a few times hoping to shame the grandparents into bringing them into the quiet room…to no avail…

Matthew 18 (KJV)
18 At the same time came the disciples unto Jesus, saying, Who is the greatest in the kingdom of heaven? 2 And Jesus called a little child unto him, and set him in the midst of them, 3 And said, Verily I say unto you, Except ye be converted, and become as little children, ye shall not enter into the kingdom of heaven. 4 Whosoever therefore shall humble himself as this little child, the same is greatest in the kingdom of heaven. 5 And whoso shall receive one such little child in my name receiveth me. 6 But whoso shall offend one of these little ones which believe in me, it were better for him that a millstone were hanged about his neck, and that he were drowned in the depth of the sea.

Dear Lord, help me to become as a little child. Help me to humble myself. Help give me more tolerance…and I pray that tonight's homily was not essential to my salvation as I could only hear every third or fourth word of it…

Day 188

I think it is great to have goals for your life. I think it is great to strive to be better today than you were yesterday but when did it become wrong to be content where you are? ...

1 Timothy 6:6-11
Now there is great gain in godliness with contentment, for we brought nothing into the world, and we cannot take anything out of the world. But if we have food and clothing, with these we will be content. But those who desire to be rich fall into temptation, into a snare, into many senseless and harmful desires that plunge people into ruin and destruction. For the love of money is a root of all kinds of evils. It is through this craving that some have wandered away from the faith and pierced themselves with many pangs.

Take time today to be grateful for what you have and Who's you are. Take a deep breath and be joyful and content in this very moment.

Day 189

April Fools Day... I'm sure God enjoys a good joke but I am equally sure they should not be crude...

Ephesians 5:3-5
3 But sexual immorality and all impurity or covetousness must not even be named among you, as is proper among saints. 4 Let there be no filthiness nor foolish talk nor crude joking, which are out of place, but instead let there be thanksgiving. 5 For you may be sure of this, that everyone who is sexually immoral or impure, or who is covetous (that is, an idolater), has no inheritance in the kingdom of Christ and God.

Keep it clean, my friends. By doing so, we honor God.

Feel like you need to make a change based upon what you just read?

Day 190

It's tough to overcome the challenges and adversity we will face in our lives by ourselves, but with Faith…

2 Corinthians 4:8-9
We are afflicted in every way, but not crushed; perplexed, but not driven to despair; persecuted, but not forsaken; struck down, but not destroyed;

…And after you have suffered a little while, the God of all grace, who has called you to his eternal glory in Christ, will himself restore, confirm, strengthen, and establish you.

Check that out… 1 Peter 5:10

Day 191

So, Christ rose from the grave yesterday and everything felt different. Today the alarm clock went off and it's just another Monday…or is it?

2 Corinthians 5:17
Therefore, if anyone is in Christ, he is a new creation. The old has passed away; behold, the new has come.

It's not just another Monday unless you let it be one. What can you do today to allow Christ to shine through you in a way that is so obvious to those around you that THEY know there is something different about this Monday?

AND

He has risen.

John 11:25-26
Jesus said to her, "I am the resurrection and the life. Whoever believes in me, though he die, yet shall he live, and everyone who lives and believes in me shall never die. Do you believe this?"

And because of that, Everything has changed.

Day 192

I was once in a Bible study group where a "doctor of theology" announced that "no one with a doctorate" could ever believe in Creation over Evolution. I calmly announced he was not the only one in the room with a doctorate...

Genesis 1:1
In the beginning God created the heavens and the earth.

Genesis 1:27
So God created mankind in his own image, in the image of God he created them; male and female he created them.

Genesis 1:31
And God saw every thing that he had made, and, behold, it was very good. And the evening and the morning were the sixth day.

"If the solar system was brought about by an accidental collision, then the appearance of organic life on this planet was also an accident, and the whole evolution of Man was an accident too. If so, then all our present thoughts are mere accidents--the accidental by-product of the movement of atoms. And this holds for the thoughts of the materialists and astronomers as well as for anyone else's. But if their thoughts--i.e. of materialism and astronomy--are merely accidental by-products, why should we believe them to be true? I see no reason for believing that one accident should be able to give me a correct account of all the other accidents." – C.S. Lewis

Day 193

While here on vacation, we went to Captain George's Seafood buffet. The Buffet is 75 yards long, about ¾ the length of a football field. People walked back to their tables with crab legs stacked a foot high as though it were their last supper. This place was one of about 12 similar buffets in town all touting all you can shove down your gullet seafood, steak and anything else your stomach desires.

Philippians 3:19 ESV
Their end is destruction, their god is their belly, and they glory in their shame, with minds set on earthly things.

1 Corinthians 10:31 ESV
So, whether you eat or drink, or whatever you do, do all to the glory of God.

So, gluttony is a pretty bad sin. People are starving in this world and we ate until we were stuffed. Somehow, we were consoled by saying grace before the meal...

Day 194

There seems to be so much discord in our world today. Instead of marching against who we hate, perhaps we could sit quietly and pray. And while we are on our knees anyway, how about we pray for those we love and thank God for all our blessings?

Proverbs 10:12
Hatred stirs up strife, but love covers all offenses.

Romans 12:17
"Never pay back evil for evil to anyone. Respect what is right in the sight of all men. If possible, so far as it depends on you, be at peace with all men"

Romans 12:19-21
Never take your own revenge, beloved, but leave room for the wrath of God, for it is written, "Vengeance is Mine, I will repay," says the Lord. "But if your enemy is hungry, feed him, and if he is thirsty, give him a drink; for in so doing you will heap burning coals on his head." Do not be overcome by evil, but overcome evil with good."

Every thing that you are against weakens you and everything that you are for empowers you.

Day 195

I am staying in a condo on vacation that has an interesting wall hanging. It is entitled: Advice from an OCEAN… Let your cares drift away…Seas every opportunity… Adapt to changing tides…Surf life's rough waves… Harbor strength & persevere… Don't be shellfish…Bet on a shore thing… *LOVE*

Psalm 55:22
Cast your cares on the LORD and he will sustain you; he will never let the righteous be shaken.
Galatians 6:10
So then, while we have opportunity, let us do good to all people, and especially to those who are of the household of the faith.
Romans 12:2
Do not be conformed to this world, but be transformed by the renewal of your mind, that by testing you may discern what is the will of God, what is good and acceptable and perfect.
Romans 8:18
For I consider that the sufferings of this present time are not worth comparing with the glory that is to be revealed to us.
Philippians 4:13
I can do all things through him who strengthens me.
1 Corinthians 10:24
Let no one seek his own good, but the good of his neighbor.
1 Timothy 6:7
For we brought nothing into this world, and it is certain we can carry nothing out. (that's about the only thing you can bet on)
1 Corinthians 16:14
Let all that you do be done in love.

Obviously each of those verses corresponds to a line of Advice From An Ocean. We can find the teachings of the Bible everywhere we look if the Word is truly on our mind, in our heart and proceeds from our lips each day.

Day 196

Have you ever felt guilty about taking time for rest and relaxation? Here's what the Bible has to say about that...

Mark 6:30-32 ESV
The apostles returned to Jesus and told him all that they had done and taught. And he said to them, "Come away by yourselves to a desolate place and rest a while." For many were coming and going, and they had no leisure even to eat. And they went away in the boat to a desolate place by themselves.

Even when we are doing God's work, we are encouraged by Jesus to go away, find a quiet place, and rest a while. In Luke 5:16 Jesus gives us a hint as to what we might do to enhance our vacation... Pray.

Day 197

I remember my coaches in high school and college used to emphasize the importance of a strong finish in winning our race or game. One coach would tell us, no matter how tired we were to "Sprint through the finish line". Another coach used to remind us that games were won in the 4th quarter.

2 Timothy 4:7
I have fought the good fight, I have finished the race, I have kept the faith.

Spiritually, I believe that the same applies. Fight the good fight, then sprint through the finish line KNOWING who is waiting for us with open arms to welcome us home.

Are you running an important race right now? What is it and how can you finish strong?

Day 198

Yesterday I talked about knowing the right thing to do, but choosing to do something else instead. Temptation goes back to Adam and Eve. They knew that they could have and do anything they wanted in the Garden of Eden except eat from the tree of knowledge. We all know how that worked out…

1 Corinthians 10:13 ESV
No temptation has overtaken you that is not common to man. God is faithful, and he will not let you be tempted beyond your ability, but with the temptation he will also provide the way of escape, that you may be able to endure it.

Most of us don't know or appreciate just how good we have it and go looking for more. Temptation is around every corner. A bigger house or car look good until we have to make the first payment. We would love to have a healthy heart and fit into that pair of jeans again until we see that awesome looking cannoli at the Italian bakery and eat two in one sitting. We may even look at the "grass" on the other side of the fence and lust for our "grass" to be that green. Temptation is inevitable but so is the strength given you by God to overcome it.

Day 199

I find the TV shows that feature "mediums" or people that can bring messages from dead relatives and friends captivating. You know, the long Island Medium, the Hollywood Medium, even back in the day the Crossing Over TV show. I must admit that some 20+ years ago I went to a medium in Cincinnati that was famous for finding lost children for the police department, Patricia Michelle. I spent several hundred dollars for 30 minutes of her time but I found her quite accurate and specific in what she shared about past, current and future events in my life and my family's life. So, what does the Bible say about all this?

1 Samuel 28:6-11
He asked the Lord what he should do, but the Lord refused to answer him, either by dreams or by sacred lots or by the prophets. Saul then said to his advisers, "Find a woman who is a medium, so I can go and ask her what to do." His advisers replied, "There is a medium at Endor." So Saul disguised himself by wearing ordinary clothing instead of his royal robes. Then he went to the woman's home at night, accompanied by two of his men. "I have to talk to a man who has died," he said. "Will you call up his spirit for me?" "Are you trying to get me killed?" the woman demanded. "You know that Saul has outlawed all the mediums and all who consult the spirits of the dead. Why are you setting a trap for me?" But Saul took an oath in the name of the Lord and promised, "As surely as the Lord lives, nothing bad will happen to you for doing this." Finally, the woman said, "Well, whose spirit do you want me to call up?" "Call up Samuel," Saul replied.

If you're not a Bible scholar, what happened next is that Saul lost his life for not waiting for an answer from God and instead consulting a medium. I must admit that on this one, I get it but I don't get it. I was only uplifted and I have seen others gain closure and resolve inner conflicts through these mediums. On the other hand, while playing with a Ouija Board in college, what I would consider to be Very dangerous and scary and evil spirit came through. I can tell you what the Bible says about this topic and it is very clear... Don't do it.
Isn't it interesting that we can be told in no uncertain terms something is bad for us and still be irresistibly drawn to do it anyway?

Day 200

God's voice is always in our lives. Sometimes we are yelled at and sometimes we must listen in silence to hear what He has to say...

For God speaks again and again, though people do not recognize it. He speaks in dreams, in visions of the night, when deep sleep falls on people as they lie in their beds. He whispers in their ears... Job 33:14-16

And sometimes He speaks to us in our dreams.

Try something fun. Put a pad and a pencil next to your bed and if you wake up in the middle of the night, jot down what messages if any you got through your dreams... don't worry, it's biblical...

Day 201

To be yourself in a world that is constantly trying to make you something else is the greatest accomplishment.- Ralph Waldo Emerson

1 John 2:15-17
Do not love the world or the things in the world. If anyone loves the world, the love of the Father is not in him. For all that is in the world—the desires of the flesh and the desires of the eyes and pride in possessions—is not from the Father but is from the world. And the world is passing away along with its desires, but whoever does the will of God abides forever.

Romans 12:2
Do not be conformed to this world, but be transformed by the renewal of your mind, that by testing you may discern what is the will of God, what is good and acceptable and perfect.

God made you absolutely amazing just the way you are, don't let this world change you. Remember, we are in this world, not of this world...don't let it suck you in and steal your uniqueness. God loves you just the way you are!

Day 202

Ever been in the presence of what my grandmother used to call a "Holy Roller"? That is what she used to call someone that is very loud and boisterous about praising God in public. It almost seems that these people are screaming out Jesus' name just to attract attention to themselves instead of quietly praising Him with their actions and deeds.

James 2:14-17 (The Message)
Does merely talking about faith indicate that a person really has it? For instance, you come upon an old friend dressed in rags and half-starved and say, "Good morning, friend! Be clothed in Christ! Be filled with the Holy Spirit!" and walk off without providing so much as a coat or a cup of soup - where does that get you? Isn't it obvious that God-talk without God-acts is outrageous nonsense?

Hey, there's nothing wrong with praising the name of Jesus out loud. But, God wants less blowhards and more doers, less conversation and more perspiration.

Day 203

I saw a T-shirt that read, "Beer is proof that God loves us and wants us to be happy." That got me thinking. Is there proof that God loves us and wants us to be happy besides beer?

1 John 4:10
In this is love, not that we have loved God but that he loved us and sent his Son to be the propitiation for our sins.

Romans 5:8
But God shows his love for us in that while we were still sinners, Christ died for us.

Philippians 4:4
Rejoice in the Lord always; again I will say, Rejoice.

God loved us so much that He sacrificed that which He loved most for us…His son. I know that I could never have sacrificed either of my kids even if I knew they would rise again in 3 days. I just couldn't have let them suffer. Just think about it. How can you doubt His love for us after contemplating that? God does indeed want us to be happy…Let us Rejoice and be happy!

Day 204

Guilt is a cognitive or an emotional experience that occurs when a person believes or realizes—accurately or not—that he or she has compromised his or her own standards of conduct or has violated a moral standard and bears significant responsibility for that violation. It is closely related to the concept of remorse. Ever felt that way?

Job 11:6
And that he would tell you the secrets of wisdom! For he is manifold in understanding. Know then that God exacts of you less than your guilt deserves.

We are called to spread the Gospel of Jesus Christ. I used to feel guilty when the person I shared the story with just didn't "get it". I have come to realize that we are called to share our faith with unconditional love, not jam it down their throat. We are called to throw a lifesaver when we see a person drowning, but it is impossible to force them to grab it.

Day 205

I had an interesting experience this morning. I wrote a heartfelt message yesterday that was well received by almost all of those that read it. Among other things, I wrote that I intend to take better care of my health, family, friends and business and spend more time in prayer and meditation. One person interpreted it as the fact that I sounded "confused". Not wanting to be judgmental, I re-read the blog with an open mind...

1 Peter 5:8
Be sober-minded; be watchful. Your adversary the devil prowls around like a roaring lion, seeking someone to devour.

Then I remembered that when you have a revelation from God, set a big goal or make an important decision, you should not share it with others. Keep it to yourself a secret and protect it. The devil will use others to cast doubt on your Godly plans. When I remembered this, I asked myself, "O you of little faith, why did you doubt?"...I think that's Biblical...

Day 206

I love the fact that Everyone has been invited to the supper of the Lord. That means that everyone is invited to the Life giving meal Jesus talked about at the last supper. At this meal, He offered us bread to spiritually represent his body which would be broken to pay for our sins and wine which would spiritually represent the blood he would spill for us to wash us clean of our transgressions. Still, many come up with Excuses as to why they can not eat of the bread or drink of the cup...

Luke 14:18-20
But they all alike began to make excuses. The first said to him, 'I have bought a field, and I must go out and see it. Please have me excused.' And another said, 'I have bought five yoke of oxen, and I go to examine them. Please have me excused.' And another said, 'I have married a wife, and therefore I cannot come.'

Excuses are like garbage cans. Everyone has one and they all stink!

Day 207

I'm a big fan of cutting to the chase. I'm the guy that read the last chapter of the mystery novel before I began the book. I like to know where we're going before we get into the car for a long drive. So if you distilled down the commandments, which ones are the really important ones?

Mark 12:30-31
30 and you shall love the Lord your God with all your heart, and with all your soul, and with all your mind, and with all your strength.' 31 The second is this, 'You shall love your neighbor as yourself.' There is no other commandment greater than these."

OK, I gave you the most important two. Doesn't it make you wonder what the rest of them are? Go ahead. Check it out. Bet you'll be glad you did!

Day 208

I had an interesting experience this morning. I wrote a heartfelt message yesterday that was well received by almost all of those that read it. Among other things, I wrote that I intend to take better care of my health, family, friends and business and spend more time in prayer and meditation. One person interpreted it as the fact that I sounded "confused". Not wanting to be judgmental, I re-read the blog with an open mind…

1 Peter 5:8
Be sober-minded; be watchful. Your adversary the devil prowls around like a roaring lion, seeking someone to devour.

Then I remembered that when you have a revelation from God, set a big goal or make an important decision, you should not share it with others. Keep it to yourself a secret and protect it. The devil will use others to cast doubt on your Godly plans. When I remembered this, I asked myself, "O you of little faith, why did you doubt?"…I think that's Biblical…

Day 209

My son's middle name is Joshua. Joshua happens to be one of my favorite books of the Bible. Contained within it's pages is this gem...

Joshua 1:9
Have I not commanded you? Be strong and courageous. Do not be frightened, and do not be dismayed, for the Lord your God is with you wherever you go."

Be Strong and Courageous, no need to be frightened or dismayed...Why? Because The Lord God Almighty, The Creator of the Universe, happens to be with YOU wherever you go. Just sit back and ruminate on that for a minute.

Day 210

I've only missed about 5 or 6 days in the office due to dis-ease (chiropractic term for illness) in the last 25 years but today I am home recovering from something that came on like a ton of bricks and overcame my immune response. I believe there is a lesson that can be learned from dis-ease.

Romans 5:3-4
More than that, we rejoice in our sufferings, knowing that suffering produces endurance, and endurance produces character, and character produces hope,

Let me tell you, it is tough to give thanks and rejoice when you are laying in bed and coughing up your lung but that is exactly what I have decided to do. I have learned the importance of giving your body rest, the power of the prayers that friends and family said for me, the kindness of my neighbor that cooked chicken soup for me, the importance of being adjusted (thank you Dr. Nicole for my adjustment and thank you Dr. Frank for offering to come from CT just to adjust me), and most importantly, the importance of choosing the right wife who will stand by and take care of you in times of sickness and trial (thank you Lori). These are the things I have learned from this dis-ease and I REJOICE and GIVE THANKS to my Lord and Savior, Jesus Christ.

Day 211

So, I had a great question asked of me by my friend yesterday. The question was related to the cross but it has bigger implications. She asked, " What are your thoughts on the bibles stance of no graven images or idols?" Immediately I thought of the ornate statues in St. Patrick's Cathedral in NYC representing many of the saints. The real danger comes if we worship the statues or the graven images…

Exodus 20:4-6 "You must not make for yourself an idol of any kind or an image of anything in the heavens or on the earth or in the sea. You must not bow down to them or worship them, for I, the Lord your God, am a jealous God who will not tolerate your affection for any other gods. I lay the sins of the parents upon their children; the entire family is affected—even children in the third and fourth generations of those who reject me. But I lavish unfailing love for a thousand generations on those who love me and obey my commands.

So, I spent a morning with a good friend who is a Catholic Priest and he explained it this way (of course I am paraphrasing and I hope I got most of this right so don't get on his case if I misquoted him here smile emoticon)… We do not worship the statue or the images or even the carving of the Cross, we merely use them to help recall the person or thing depicted. God doesn't prohibit the making of statues or images of various creatures for religious purposes (cf. 1 Kgs. 6:29–32, 8:6–66; 2 Chr. 3:7–14). If God did prohibit them then we would have to destroy all the Pictures of Jesus and other biblical persons appearing on a myriad of Bibles, picture books, T-shirts, jewelry, bumper stickers, greeting cards, compact discs, and manger scenes. Christ is even symbolically represented through the Icthus or "fish emblem." Bottom line, bow down and worship God, not stuff that represents Him or any other religious person or thing. The cross may be in front of you as you go to bended knee, but it is God that we are bowing down before, not any graven image or idol.

Day 212

The cross is a symbol. It can be a symbol of a gruesome death. It can be the symbol of sacrifice for you and me. It can be the symbol of unconditional love. It can be a symbol of triumph. It can be a symbol of forgiveness. The cross evokes so many emotions for the Christian. What does the Bible say about the cross?

1 Peter 2:22-24 (AMP)
22 HE COMMITTED NO SIN, NOR WAS DECEIT EVER FOUND IN HIS MOUTH. 23 While being reviled and insulted, He did not revile or insult in return; while suffering, He made no threats [of vengeance], but kept entrusting Himself to Him who judges fairly. 24 He personally carried our sins in His body on the cross [willingly offering Himself on it, as on an altar of sacrifice], so that we might die to sin [becoming immune from the penalty and power of sin] and live for righteousness; for by His wounds you [who believe] have been healed.

Through Christ's death on the cross, those who turn to Him are delivered from both the penalty and the power of sin. Sit quietly in prayer and contemplate what the cross symbolizes for YOU.

Day 213

Have you ever been doing something as a routine, over and over again and felt it was getting boring? Waking at the same time, working out, doing chores, a task at work, maybe even prayer?Often a routine can start to feel like a rut but David and Daniel understood the importance of a routine...

Psalm 5:3
My voice shalt thou hear in the morning, O Lord; in the morning will I direct my prayer unto thee, and will look up.

Daniel 6:10
10 Now when Daniel knew that the writing was signed, he went into his house; and his windows being open in his chamber toward Jerusalem, he kneeled upon his knees three times a day, and prayed, and gave thanks before his God, as he did aforetime.

David's routine was to wake early in the morning every day to praise God, he knew it was the best time for him to speak with God. What Daniel did to continue his routine of praying 3 times on bent knee doesn't seem like a big deal until you realize that the writing that was signed was a law that required you be thrown into a pit of hungry lions as penalty for praying to God. Though you may feel like you are in a rut, some routines give meaning to Life and are even worth dying for.

Day 214

So, what's in a name? Particularly, God's name?...

Exodus 3:13-15
Then Moses said to God, "If I come to the people of Israel and say to them, 'The God of your fathers has sent me to you,' and they ask me, 'What is his name?' what shall I say to them?" God said to Moses, "I am who I am." And he said, "Say this to the people of Israel, 'I am has sent me to you.'" God also said to Moses, "Say this to the people of Israel, 'The Lord, the God of your fathers, the God of Abraham, the God of Isaac, and the God of Jacob, has sent me to you.' This is my name forever, and thus I am to be remembered throughout all generations.

Biblically, there are literally hundreds of names for God. For me, in the end God is Abba (my father) and Agape Love (unconditional love). Power in the name? Listen to this and see if it stirs your spirit or lifts the hair on your arm just hearing God's name spoken...

Day 215

As we search for meaning and try to solve the mysteries of life, the Bible often teaches us that things are not what they appear.

Luke 14:11
For all those who exalt themselves will be humbled, and those who humble themselves will be exalted."

This is part of the great reversal. The humble will be exalted. The last shall be first. The way to get what we need is to give more of that thing away. Listen, in the natural, this does not make sense but in the spiritual, it makes perfect sense. Have you sat quietly reading the Bible or in prayer lately?

Day 216

My friend Jim is a pastor and wrote an article about "praying scared". It got me thinking that I very seldom pray out of fear any more. I'm not even scared of dying or the end of times. I am completely at peace even though I have put my request in to have 120 years here in this body to serve Him. Jesus said that the end of time will come like a thief in the night and no one will know the time or the day.

Matthew 24:36-44
"But of that day and hour no one knows, not even the angels of heaven, nor the Son, but the Father alone. For the coming of the Son of Man will be just like the days of Noah. For as in those days before the flood they were eating and drinking, marrying and giving in marriage, until the day that Noah entered the ark, and they did not understand until the flood came and took them all away; so will the coming of the Son of Man be. Then there will be two men in the field; one will be taken and one will be left. Two women will be grinding at the mill; one will be taken and one will be left."

One thing is for sure, even though we may not know the day or the time, we are always one day closer to the end. Are we approaching that day with Joy and Anticipation of what's to come or are we fearing it and "praying scared"?

Day 217

When we are confronted with a difficult decision we have two choices: React or Respond. The answer when we react is either YES or NO. When we respond the answer is Maybe or I will have to Pray on that and get back to you later.

Proverbs 12:15
The way of a fool is right in his own eyes, but a wise man listens to advice.

Proverbs 11:14
Where there is no guidance, a people falls, but in an abundance of counselors there is safety.

Proverbs 19:20-21
Listen to advice and accept instruction, that you may gain wisdom in the future. Many are the plans in the mind of a man, but it is the purpose of the Lord that will stand.

Yesterday many of you gave me wise counsel. For that I am grateful. I pray that we are moved to Respond instead of React in the future so that we can seek wise counsel when possible both from friends and family as well as from God in prayer. Have a blessed day!

Day 218

I learned a valuable lesson yesterday from a patient. We had a disagreement. She felt I had an obligation to sit and listen to all her symptoms and personal problems for 15 minutes while a waiting room full of people sat patiently for their life giving chiropractic adjustment and I felt she should get on the table to let me do my job or she should perhaps seek out another chiropractor that better suited her needs. She then sarcastically exclaimed, "You think you're a Christian?"

Romans 5:1
Therefore, having been justified by faith, we have peace with God through our Lord Jesus Christ,

20 people in my reception room were glad I didn't spend 15-20 minutes in the room with her but I wonder if I would have spent that time sitting and listening if it were Jesus in that room asking for my time. Here is what I know for certain: I am a child of The Lord God Almighty and I am saved through the Grace provided to me by the sacrifice His Son made for me. No one can cause me to doubt that. Don't let anyone including Satan cause you to ever doubt that. God doesn't make promises that He can't keep.

Day 219

Baptism can be so confusing. Each Christian religion thinks they have the rules "down pat". Sprinkle with water, submerge in water, the water must be sprinkled while saying this, no you must be in a white robe, but it doesn't count if you're not in a specific church, etc. When did we get so legalistic and so off course thinking these rules were more important than the simple pure act of baptism as an act of Faith?

Acts 8:36-38
And as they were going along the road they came to some water, and the eunuch said, "See, here is water! What prevents me from being baptized?" And he commanded the chariot to stop, and they both went down into the water, Philip and the eunuch, and he baptized him.

Matthew 28:19-20
Go therefore and make disciples of all nations, baptizing them in the name of the Father and of the Son and of the Holy Spirit, teaching them to observe all that I have commanded you. And behold, I am with you always, to the end of the age."

Baptism can and should be a beautiful, simple and profound moment in a Christian's life. No legalistic rules, no fanfare, just a desire to repent of our sins and a welcoming of Jesus into our hearts to be our Lord and Savior. I was blessed to be able to baptize my brother in the name of the Father, the Son and the Holy Spirit. I am confident his sins were washed away that afternoon and he received the Holy Spirit.

Day 220

Do you know what every successful person has in common?

Colossians 1:9-10
And so, from the day we heard, we have not ceased to pray for you, asking that you may be filled with the knowledge of his will in all spiritual wisdom and understanding, so as to walk in a manner worthy of the Lord, fully pleasing to him, bearing fruit in every good work and increasing in the knowledge of God.

…They have someone that is praying for them.

Day 221

It has been bitterly cold here for the last two days. There doesn't seem to be anything good that can come of it but it too comes from God.

Job 37:10
"From the breath of God ice is made, And the expanse of the waters is frozen.

After thinking for a minute, if it came from God, there must be some good in it. Then I thought about all those people that suffer from allergies and how they only get relief when everything freezes over. A hard freeze has a cleansing effect on nature though it is bitter to take at times.

Day 222

There's a war between guilt and grace and they're fighting for a sacred space
but I'm living proof grace wins every time…

For the prodigal son (Luke 15:11-32)
Grace wins

For the woman at the well (John 4:4-26)
Grace wins

For the blind man and the beggar (Mark 8:22-25 and Luke 18:35-43)
Grace wins

For always and forever (Hebrews 13:8)
Grace wins

For the lost out on the streets (Colossians 4:5)
Grace wins

For the worst part of you and me (1 John 1:9)
Grace wins

For the thief on the cross (Luke 23:43)
Grace wins

For a world that is lost (Luke 19:10)
Grace wins

No more lying down in death's defeat now I'm rising up in victory
Singing, hallelujah, grace wins every time.

Day 223

I love the term and the very idea of the Shekinah Glory of God. Just say it out loud...Shekinah Glory! It is the majestic presence or manifestation of God in which He descends to dwell among men. Whenever the invisible God becomes visible, and whenever the omnipresence of God is localized, this is the Shechinah Glory.

Exodus 24:16-18
The glory of the LORD rested on Mount Sinai, and the cloud covered it for six days; and on the seventh day He called to Moses from the midst of the cloud. And to the eyes of the sons of Israel the appearance of the glory of the LORD was like a consuming fire on the mountain top. Moses entered the midst of the cloud as he went up to the mountain; and Moses was on the mountain forty days and forty nights.

In the Old Testament, most of these visible manifestations took the form of light, fire, or cloud, or a combination of these. A new form appears in the New Testament: the Incarnate Word [John 1:14]. Next time you pray, notice the Shekinah Glory that is with you. PS- It's OK to be overwhelmed by His presence.

Day 224

I am sitting here listening to a presidential debate. Frankly, they all disappoint me. I've listened to the other party's candidates fight among themselves as well. So, how can we know who to vote for?

1 Timothy 3:1-7
The saying is trustworthy: If anyone aspires to the office of overseer, he desires a noble task. Therefore an overseer must be above reproach, the husband of one wife, sober-minded, self-controlled, respectable, hospitable, able to teach, not a drunkard, not violent but gentle, not quarrelsome, not a lover of money. He must manage his own household well, with all dignity keeping his children submissive, for if someone does not know how to manage his own household, how will he care for God's church? ...

Loyal, Sober, Composed, Courteous, Honest, Honorable, Trustworthy, Considerate, Good Natured, Faithful, Lover of God not Money, Guardian, Servant... When we cast our vote, these are the qualities that Christians should be looking for remembering that there is no one that is perfect.

Day 225

Ever felt torn about making an important decision? You know the right and moral thing to do but you think something else will bring more pleasure? Here is some important advice from the Word...

Matthew 26:41
Watch and pray, that ye enter not into temptation: the spirit indeed is willing, but the flesh is weak.

Romans 8:3-4
For God has done what the law, weakened by the flesh, could not do. By sending his own Son in the likeness of sinful flesh and for sin, he condemned sin in the flesh, in order that the righteous requirement of the law might be fulfilled in us, who walk not according to the flesh but according to the Spirit.

There's always going to be a battle between the spirit and the flesh. The Bible acknowledges that (Ecclesiastes 7:20). I guess it all boils down to a phrase my parents used when we asked for advice hoping they would say "B" when we knew the right answer was "A"...It's your choice but Do The Right Thing.

Day 226

It's funny how we crave second chances when we've done something wrong but when someone does something to us, when they really upset us or have directly and intentionally ignored our advice, it's so tough to forgive them and just "let it go"...

Matthew 18:21-22
Then Peter came up and said to him, "Lord, how often will my brother sin against me, and I forgive him? As many as seven times?" Jesus said to him, "I do not say to you seven times, but seventy times seven.

To Err is human, to Forgive, to really and truly FORGIVE is divine. Who have you not given the gift of forgiveness to and welcomed back with open arms yet? Lord God, please give us the strength, wisdom and ability to forgive those that have trespassed against us as you have forgiven us our trespasses.

Day 227

I think it's wrong to ask, "What does it cost to encourage one another?"
That's the rhetorical question I was going to ask to start this morning's
study…

1 Thessalonians 5:11
Therefore encourage one another and build one another up, just as you are
doing.

Hebrews 10:25
Not neglecting to meet together, as is the habit of some, but encouraging
one another, and all the more as you see the Day drawing near.

Instead, we should meditate and pray on the question, "What might it cost if
we don not encourage one another?" Be ready to share good news and to
build one another up at a moment's notice. Be slow to anger, to criticize,
and to judge today as we seek first to understand completely before we seek
to be understood.

Day 228

I have been trying to choose healthier foods to eat in an effort to become healthier over all. It's true that your body is the "temple of God" and as such, you should only put things into the temple that are good and acceptable to Him.

Mark 7:15-19
There is nothing outside a person that by going into him can defile him, but the things that come out of a person are what defile him." And when he had entered the house and left the people, his disciples asked him about the parable. And he said to them, "Then are you also without understanding? Do you not see that whatever goes into a person from outside cannot defile him, since it enters not his heart but his stomach, and is expelled?"

(Thus he declared all foods clean.)
As it turns out, it's not so much what goes in that's important. It's what comes out…

Day 229

Have you ever heard that little voice within speaking to you? Ever wonder if you should listen to it? Is it a message from God or is it the enemy or your ego trying to tempt you to do something? How can you know the difference?

1 John 4:1
Beloved, do not believe every spirit, but test the spirits to see whether they are from God, for many false prophets have gone out into the world.

Hebrews 5:14
But solid food is for the mature, for those who have their powers of discernment trained by constant practice to distinguish good from evil.

Wondering if you should listen to that small voice within? Test what it's saying against the Truth found in the Bible. The only way to discern the truth from a lie is to study the Truth.

Day 230

I once read a book by Dr. Norman Vincent Peal called The Power of Positive Thinking. In the book he talked about Tranquility. It really is a very interesting word. Just saying this melodic word out loud seems to have a calming effect on the body.

Philippians 4:6
Do not be anxious about anything, but in everything by prayer and supplication with thanksgiving let your requests be made known to God.

In a state of Tranquility, we need not be anxious about anything. Through the Word, prayer and supplication, in a state of gratitude, if we just sit quietly with God, Tranquility is ours.

Day 231

I've heard people say many times that the God of the Old Testament is so much different than the God of the New Testament. I have read the Bible front to back several times and I have to say that I disagree. When it is read all together, it is really an historical account of a Father and his relationship with His children over the course of time. It is really a love story…

Exodus 34:6
6 The Lord passed before him and proclaimed, "The Lord, the Lord, a God merciful and gracious, slow to anger, and abounding in steadfast love and faithfulness,

Romans 1:18
18 For the wrath of God is revealed from heaven against all ungodliness and unrighteousness of men, who by their unrighteousness suppress the truth.

Ironically, often we find God to be a loving and kind God in the Old Testament and serving up perfect justice in the New Testament. The truth is that God is not different from one testament to another and that God's wrath and His love are revealed in both testaments. He is One God and there is One Truth contained in One Bible which happens to be divided into two parts.

James 1:17
17 Every good gift and every perfect gift is from above, coming down from the Father of lights with whom there is no variation or shadow due to change.

Day 232

I think at one time or another we have all thought to ourselves, "Maybe I would be better off without Facebook. Maybe my time would be better spent elsewhere." Well, in this age of "selfies" and "facebook friends" a plenty whom we have never met in person, you will be surprised to know that there is advice from God in His Word about the pitfalls of this new phenomenon…

As for Facebook friends: Proverbs 18:24
A man of many companions may come to ruin, but there is a friend who sticks closer than a brother.

As for people's advice and opinions on Facebook: 2 Timothy 4:3 (AMP)
3 For the time will come when people will not tolerate sound doctrine and accurate instruction [that challenges them with God's Truth]; but wanting to have their ears tickled [with something pleasing], they will accumulate for themselves [many] teachers [one after another, chosen] to satisfy their own desires and to support the errors they hold,

And as for Selfies on Facebook: 1 Samuel 16:7 (NASB)
7 But the Lord said to Samuel, "Do not look at his appearance or at the height of his stature, because I have rejected him; for God sees not as man sees, for man looks at the outward appearance, but the Lord looks at the heart."

Don't be fooled into believing your true friends are found in cyberland on Facebook. Don't be fooled into believing that what you read on Facebook is the Truth. Don't look at someone's selfie and judge them or compare yourself to them, only God knows what is in the heart. Do trust in God, Go to Him in Prayer and read His Word. Ok, what are you waiting for? Shut off this computer and do it.

Day 233

I have been ruminating on the word Coward and what it really means. As it turns out, it's not such a cool thing in the Bible. It is right up there with unbeliever, murderer, sorcerer, idolater, occultist, and liar…

Revelation 21:7-8 (AMP)
7 He who overcomes [the world by adhering faithfully to Christ Jesus as Lord and Savior] will inherit these things, and I will be his God and he will be My son. 8 But as for the cowards and unbelieving and abominable [who are devoid of character and personal integrity and practice or tolerate immorality], and murderers, and sorcerers [with intoxicating drugs], and idolaters and occultists [who practice and teach false religions], and all the liars [who knowingly deceive and twist truth], their part will be in the lake that blazes with fire and brimstone, which is the second death."

As a follower of Jesus Christ, we must adhere to His Word faithfully. We are overcomers. We are the sons and daughters of God. (Proverbs 28:1) The wicked flee when no one pursues, but the righteous are bold as a lion. (Proverbs 29:25) The fear of man lays a snare, but whoever trusts in the Lord is safe. As the sons and daughters of God, we can be bold as a lion and know that we are safe from all the fear the enemy can dole out.

Day 234

My daughter is a very wise young woman. She said she was troubled by the Biblical instruction to "fear" the Lord. She told me that if God is Love, isn't it CRAZY to fear LOVE? She asked, "As a father, do you want me to FEAR you?" Of course I don't, I desire to be loved and respected. So, what does the Bible really mean by Fear the Lord?

Greek and Hebrew words translated as "fear" in the Bible have several different meanings:
The Hebrew verb yare can mean "to fear, to respect, to reverence" and the Hebrew noun yirah "usually refers to the fear of God and is viewed as a positive quality. This fear acknowledges God's good intentions (Ex. 20:20) and makes a person receptive to wisdom and knowledge (Prov. 1:7; 9:10).

The Greek noun phobos can mean "reverential fear" of God, or a wholesome dread of displeasing Him. This is the type of positive, productive fear Luke describes in the early New Testament Church: "Then the churches throughout all Judea, Galilee, and Samaria had peace and were edified. And walking in the fear of the Lord and in the comfort of the Holy Spirit, they were multiplied" (Acts 9:31).

Our home was filled with love as we raised the children but we had rules like never touch the stove, don't cross the street without looking both ways, and don't stick anything into the electrical outlets. The consequences for those, among other things, were SEVERE and I got LOUD in what appeared to be anger. They FEARED ever doing those things again but I did not yell out of anger, I did it out of LOVE. That healthy fear of disobeying me, I hope was the beginning of wisdom for them. I believe the fear of God is the same.

Day 235

I really like it when I leave a store or part from a friend and they say, "Have a blessed day." I don't know about you, but I can use all the blessings I can get!

Genesis 12:2-3
2 And I will make you a great nation,
And I will bless you,
And make your name great;
And so you shall be a blessing;
3 And I will bless those who bless you,
And the one who curses you I will curse.
And in you all the families of the earth will be blessed."

…"And I will bless those who bless you"… looks like it's time to start looking for more people to bless. It's just like everything else. Whatever you want more of, give more of it away. That may not make sense in the natural, but it most definitely makes sense in the spiritual!

Day 236

Will power. Not an area I shine in particularly when it comes to food. I started thinking; will power is really part of the gift God gave us called free will. Sometimes I just wish I had no free will and I just did the right thing all the time according to God's will...

James 1:14-16
But each person is tempted when he is lured and enticed by his own desire. Then desire when it has conceived gives birth to sin, and sin when it is fully grown brings forth death. Do not be deceived, my beloved brothers.

1 Corinthians 10:13
No temptation has overtaken you that is not common to man. God is faithful, and he will not let you be tempted beyond your ability, but with the temptation he will also provide the way of escape, that you may be able to endure it.

Temptation and desires are common and we are not alone. Additionally, when we are tempted, God has already provided a way to overcome the temptation and do the right thing as well as a way to be forgiven when we make the wrong decision. OK, I guess free will isn't that bad after all. Hopefully, the more we pray and read the Word, the more our "free will" will be aligned with the will of God anyway.

Day 237

Not every day will be perfect. When you fall, rise again. Persistence alone is omnipotent.

Galatians 6:9
And let us not grow weary of doing good, for in due season we will reap, if we do not give up.

per·sist·ence pər'sistəns/Submit noun
firm or obstinate continuance in a course of action in spite of difficulty or opposition.
om·nip·o·tent ˌäm'nipəd(ə)nt/ adjective
1. having unlimited power; able to do anything.

Day 238

There was a whole lot of LOVE at the Dynamic Essentials Chiropractic conference this weekend. There seems to be a movement in our profession to become a good and loving servant to be able to help the dying, crying, suffering people in our community that are living in fear...

1 John 4:18
There is no fear in love; but perfect love casts out fear...
But how do we become Perfect Love??? The answer is simpler than you think...

Matthew 7:7
"Ask, and it will be given to you; seek, and you will find; knock, and it will be opened to you.

Reflect for a moment on how you have been a good and loving servant. Is there something more you wish you would have done? What are you waiting for?

Day 239

I am at a Chiroprac-TIC conference this weekend. I value the Fellowship found here. We gain so much from hanging out with people who are like minded but have so much information to share to help us grow. It is good to receive when we fellowship and it is just as important to share what we know to help others.

1 Thessalonians 5:11
Therefore encourage one another and build one another up, just as you are doing.

Hebrews 10: 24-25
And let us consider how to stir up one another to love and good works, Not neglecting to meet together, as is the habit of some, but encouraging one another, and all the more as you see the Day drawing near.

Ecclesiastes 4:9-12
Two are better than one, because they have a good reward for their toil. For if they fall, one will lift up his fellow. But woe to him who is alone when he falls and has not another to lift him up! Again, if two lie together, they keep warm, but how can one keep warm alone? And though a man might prevail against one who is alone, two will withstand him—a threefold cord is not quickly broken.

Proverbs 27:17
Iron sharpens iron, and one man sharpens another.

Fellowship is Biblically important. When and if you fall, isn't it good to know that someone will be there to lift you up? How valuable is it to have love and good works stirred up within you by those you fellowship with? Who are YOU fellowshipping with?

Day 240

I am amused when people ask, regarding the Hokey Pokey, "What if that IS all it is about?" I thought it was high time I did a study on LOVE in honor of being at DE, a chiropractic conference that focuses on the importance of Loving abundantly…

1 John 4:18
There is no fear in love, but perfect love casts out fear. For fear has to do with punishment, and whoever fears has not been perfected in love.

1 Corinthians 13:4-7 & 13
Love is patient and kind; love does not envy or boast; it is not arrogant or rude. It does not insist on its own way; it is not irritable or resentful; it does not rejoice at wrongdoing, but rejoices with the truth. Love bears all things, believes all things, hopes all things, endures all things… So now faith, hope, and love abide, these three; but the greatest of these is love.

Don't try to love, don't pretend to love, don't look for love outside yourself…Be Love. That's not easy, it takes dedication and present time consciousness…but in the end, it will be worth it. I'm pretty sure Love is what it is all about...

Day 241

Ever get into an argument? You know you are right and you are sure that THEY are wrong! You are Pissed and want them to admit they are wrong and apologize. Before you fly off the handle, take a breath and listen to this…

Ephesians 4:31-5:2
Let all bitterness and wrath and anger and clamor and slander be put away from you, along with all malice. Be kind to one another, tenderhearted, forgiving one another, as God in Christ forgave you. Therefore be imitators of God, as beloved children. And walk in love, as Christ loved us and gave himself up for us, a fragrant offering and sacrifice to God.

1 Corinthians 6:7
To have lawsuits at all with one another is already a defeat for you. Why not rather suffer wrong? Why not rather be defrauded?

Alright, LET IT GO! Avenge not yourselves, but rather give place unto wrath: for it is written, Vengeance is mine; I will repay, saith the Lord. (I'm pretty sure that advice is Biblical) To err is human, to forgive is divine. (pretty sure that's not Biblical but it is still pretty cool anyway).

Day 242

I had a friend ask about confession. He was wondering why Christians teach that you must confess your sins when all sins of the believer are forgiven. He also asked if we had to confess our sins to one another or just to God in prayer. I thought that deserved some prayer and study… This turns out to be a little bit more complicated than I thought…

1 John 1:9
If we confess our sins, he is faithful and just to forgive us our sins and to cleanse us from all unrighteousness.
John 20:21-24
Jesus said to them again, "Peace be with you. As the Father has sent me, even so I am sending you." And when he had said this, he breathed on them and said to them, "Receive the Holy Spirit. If you forgive the sins of any, they are forgiven them; if you withhold forgiveness from any, it is withheld."
1 Kings 8:30
Hear the supplication of your servant and of your people Israel when they pray toward this place. Hear from heaven, your dwelling place, and when you hear, forgive.
1 Timothy 2:5
For there is one God, and there is one mediator between God and men, the man Christ Jesus,

So, Biblically, confessing any of 4 different ways is A-OK. First, In the old Testament verse above, clearly you can ask God directly for forgiveness by going to Him in prayer. Second, In the New Testament, we are encouraged to confess to "one another" which not only affords the chance of forgiveness but also allows for the important opportunity to fulfill the part of the Lords prayer instructing us to "forgive those that have trespassed against us". Third, we can go to God with confession through Jesus as well since He is the only mediator between God and man. Fourth, in the New Testament, when Jesus died on the cross for us, the temple veil was torn signifying that we no longer needed to go through the chief priests to speak with God so going directly to Him in prayer is still OK. Having said that, confessing to a priest also works biblically because it still fulfills the command to confess to one another. Sorry that was so long! What I found was not what I expected, but there it is. In the final analysis- confess, repent, be forgiven and try to sin no more any biblical way you think you can get that done. Let's pray for each other!

Day 243

As we go through life, we will pass through valleys on the way to the mountain tops. Figuratively, those valleys are times of adversity. In those times, we must draw close to God and find shelter in His Word and the promises found within it.

The prophet Jeremiah wrote in Lamentations 3:22-24 KJV:
"It is of the LORD's mercies that we are not consumed, because his compassions fail not. They are new every morning: great is thy faithfulness. The LORD is my portion, saith my soul; therefore will I hope in him.

As a fan of C.S. Lewis, I like this quote about adversity: "The long, dull, monotonous years of middle-aged prosperity or middle-aged adversity are excellent campaigning weather for the devil." We are all servants. It is in adversity that we discover who we are truly serving...God or the devil...

Day 244

Last night I went to church with my wife and the church was about 80% less busy. You see, God was competing with the Patriot's football playoff game and, after all, we are New Englanders. That made me think about priorities...

Matthew 22:37-38
And he said to him, "You shall love the Lord your God with all your heart and with all your soul and with all your mind. This is the great and first commandment.

Just a few short years ago, I would have been the one glued in front of the TV instead of at church. I wonder how many people would have been in church last night had it been the Super Bowl 50 night? I wonder if I would have been there had the Super Bowl been on? (...probably not.)

Let us search ourselves today and begin to reprioritize our lives to heal our soul, mind and body.

Day 245

In Christ alone my hope is found
He is my light, my strength, my song
This CORNERSTONE, this solid ground
Firm through the fiercest drought and storm
What heights of love, what depths of peace
When fears are stilled, when strivings cease
My Comforter, my All in All
Here in the love of Christ I stand

Acts 4:10-12
let it be known to all of you and to all the people of Israel, that by the name
of Jesus Christ the Nazarene, whom you crucified, whom God raised from
the dead--by this name this man stands here before you in good health. "He
is the stone which was rejected by you, the builders, but which became the
chief CORNERSTONE." And there is salvation in no one else; for there is
no other name under heaven that has been given among men by which we
must be saved."

No guilt in life, no fear in death, this is the power of Christ in me.

Day 246

The opposite of Trust is to Doubt. Often we are caused by the enemy and worldly circumstances to doubt that God will "pull through" for us.

Psalm 37:3-5
Trust in the LORD and do good.
Then you will live safely in the land and prosper.
Take delight in the LORD,
and he will give you your heart's desires.
Commit everything you do to the LORD.
Trust him, and he will help you.

Continue to Trust God's Plan. Often the circumstances we are going through right now may seem horrible and painful but in the end, they may have a bigger purpose for us. It is from the worst things that happen to us in our lives that the best gifts in life appear. Or at least that is what I have found...

Can you recall something bad that happened in your life that God has turned around into something good in your life?

Day 247

I know a place, where we can go, to lay the troubles down eating your soul.
I know a place, where mercy flows, take the stains make you whiter than
snow…

Acts 2:38
And Peter said to them, "Repent and be baptized every one of you in the
name of Jesus Christ for the forgiveness of your sins, and you will receive
the gift of the Holy Spirit.

We're goin down to the river, down to the river, down to the river to pray.
Let's get washed by the water, washed by the water, and rise up in amazing
grace. Let's go down, down, down to the river… You will leave changed!

(Jordan Feliz - The River)

Day 248

Well, I live in the Northeast; I suppose it had to happen eventually. We got our first dusting of snow last night. I took a moment this morning to pray that my family and friends will be protected from slips and falls. Actually, the Bible has some advice about that…

Psalm 37:31
The law of their God is in their hearts; their feet do not slip.

Psalm 18:33
He makes me as surefooted as a deer,
enabling me to stand on mountain heights.

Psalm 37:23-24
23 The Lord makes firm the steps
of the one who delights in him;
24 though he may stumble, he will not fall,
for the Lord upholds him with his hand.

OK, so this will be a safe day for us all. Put God in your heart and uphold the Lord and you will be sure footed. That's easy!

Day 249

I have a friend who loves the word Jubilee. Jubilee…it's an uplifting word, isn't it? It actually means a year of emancipation and restoration, celebrated every fifty years. Emancipation is the freeing from slavery. Jubliee, I just can't stop saying it now too…

Leviticus 25:
10And you shall consecrate the fiftieth year, and proclaim liberty throughout all the land to all its inhabitants. It shall be a Jubilee for you; and each of you shall return to his possession, and each of you shall return to his family.
13'In this Year of Jubilee, each of you shall return to his possession. (be freed from slavery)

Jubilee is grace showing up in the Old Testament. Jubilee is Freedom from slavery when it is not earned or deserved. Jubilee is restoration when we are broken and hurting. How lucky are we that we don't have to wait 50 years for Jubilee? Jesus brought a Jubilee that is available 24/7, 365 days a year! This truly is our year of Jubilee!

What do you hope for in your year of Jubilee?

Day 250

God is offering an invitation to Abundant Life that requires no money?
How can that be?

Isaiah 55
1"Ho! Everyone who thirsts,
Come to the waters;
And you who have no money,
Come, buy and eat.
Yes, come, buy wine and milk
Without money and without price.
2 Why do you spend money for what is not bread,
And your wages for what does not satisfy?
Listen carefully to Me, and eat what is good,
And let your soul delight itself in abundance.
3 Incline your ear, and come to Me.
Hear, and your soul shall live;
And I will make an everlasting covenant with you—
8 "For My thoughts are not your thoughts,
Nor are your ways My ways," says the Lord.
11 So shall My word be that goes forth from My mouth;
It shall not return to Me void,
But it shall accomplish what I please,
And it shall prosper in the thing for which I sent it.
12 "For you shall go out with joy,
And be led out with peace;

I wonder if those that seek to be wealthy realize that the truly important
things in life can not be purchased with money. True abundance, joy and
peace come from the Word of God (the Bible). That may not make sense in
this messed up world but God's ways are not our ways.

Day 251

This weekend I decided to embark on a journey (literally and figuratively) to find out how to increase my Capacity. I am seeking a way to increase my capacity to help people in my office but I think we all wish we could increase our capacity… our capacity to Love, to Give, to Serve and to Receive His blessings.

1 John 4:7-8
7 Dear friends, let us continue to love one another, for love comes from God. Anyone who loves is a child of God and knows God. 8 But anyone who does not love does not know God, for God is love.

The only way to increase our capacity to do Anything is to increase our capacity to Love. It's so simple really. God is love and when we are in God's Word more, literally IN love more, we increase our capacity to be able to do All Things. Know God, Be Love and this will expand Your Capacity to Give, Serve and yes, also to receive more of His Blessings in our life.

Having said that, in Ecclesiastes 5:18-20, roughly, it advises that we should make the most of what God gives, both the bounty and the capacity to enjoy it, accepting what's given and delighting in the work. It's God's gift! Perhaps, instead of seeking more capacity under the guise of wanting to serve God more, we should accept the gifts He has given us in the present and when He feels we are ready to be stewards of more, He will give us both an increase and the Capacity to handle it.

Day 252

Well, there was a lot of talk about the 400 Million dollar lottery in the office yesterday and I suppose there will be even more talk about it now that it will be 800 Million dollars or so. One of my friends made the comment that winning lotteries makes you become who you have always been (it merely magnifies who you already are). Another friend asked, "If you win, What would you do with it and Why?"

Luke 21:1-4
And He looked up and saw the rich putting their gifts into the treasury. And He saw a poor widow putting in two small copper coins. And He said,"Truly I say to you, this poor widow put in more than all of them; for they all out of their surplus put into the offering; but she out of her poverty put in all that she had to live on."

Matthew 19:16-22
And someone came to Him and said, "Teacher, what good thing shall I do that I may obtain eternal life?"... if you wish to enter into life, keep the commandments."... "All these things I have kept; what am I still lacking?" Jesus said to him, "If you wish to be complete, go and sell your possessions and give to the poor, and you will have treasure in heaven; and come, follow Me." But when the young man heard this statement, he went away grieving; for he was one who owned much property.

Also check out Matthew 25:14-30 The Parable of the Talents

WHAT to do with the money is not easy. It seems the Bible encourages us to be good stewards of our money, being sure to tithe from the first fruits, save a portion of our money for a "rainy day", and make good investments but, in order to truly be rich, we must give it all away. WHY? Because what we have now doesn't hold a candle to what is to come IF we follow Him.

Day 253

If God already forgave us for our sins, why should we change our ways and do good instead of sinning? I mean we're forgiven already, right?... Well, that's not entirely right...

John 8:3-11

3 The scribes and the Pharisees brought a woman caught in adultery, and having set her in the center of the court, 4 they said to Him, "Teacher, this woman has been caught in adultery, in the very act. 5 Now in the Law Moses commanded us to stone such women; what then do You say?"... "He who is without sin among you, let him be the first to throw a stone at her." 8 Again He stooped down and wrote on the ground. 9 When they heard it, they began to go out one by one, beginning with the older ones, and He was left alone, and the woman, where she was, in the center of the court. 10 Straightening up, Jesus said to her, "Woman, where are they? Did no one condemn you?" 11 She said, "No one, Lord." And Jesus said, "I do not condemn you, either. Go. FROM NOW ON SIN NO MORE."

We are forgiven our sins but God admonishes us to "Go and sin no more." When we totally love God, it demonstrates our Faith. Our Faith creates our Works and our Works Complete our Faith. Know that when you screw up (which we will) God still loves us and does not condemn us.

Day 254

There will be some good days in our lives and there will be some bad days. There will be some Phenomenal days that you wish would never end and there will be some terrible days that seem like they will never end.

Ecclesiastes 7:14 (MSG)
14 On a good day, enjoy yourself;
On a bad day, examine your conscience.
God arranges for both kinds of days
So that we won't take anything for granted.

God doesn't ask us to just be thankful for the good things, He calls us to be thankful for ALL things. That is a Tall order!! Examine my conscience on a bad day? The definition of conscience is an inner feeling or voice viewed as acting as a guide to the rightness or wrongness of one's behavior.

Why do you suppose God wants us to examine our conscience on the bad days?

Day 255

I think we all get caught up in our daily routines and forget to count all the blessings in our lives.

Psalm 103:2-5
Let all that I am praise the LORD; may I never forget the good things he does for me. He forgives all my sins and heals all my diseases. He redeems me from death and crowns me with love and tender mercies. He fills my life with good things. My youth is renewed like the eagle's!

What are the good things God has done for you? Think about them, name them one by one.

Day 256

Time management…My Fraternity uses a tool called the 24 inch gauge as an analogy. It is a measuring tool that is divided into 24 equal parts symbolic of the 24 hours in a day. It folds into 3 sections of 8 inches each and reminds us to divide our day into three equal parts; whereby are found eight hours for the service of God and a distressed brother or their widow; eight hours for their usual vocations; and eight for refreshment and sleep.

Ephesians 5:15-17
Look carefully then how you walk, not as unwise but as wise, making the best use of the time, because the days are evil. Therefore do not be foolish, but understand what the will of the Lord is.

Time is man's greatest mystery, bitterest enemy, truest friend! Its care, conservation and employment, is the secret of the twenty-four inch gauge. Time wasted and aimlessly spent is not what God admonishes us to do. Remember there is also another symbolic tool many of us recognize, the Scythe, the emblem of time which always wins in the end. When the scythe arrives at our doorstep, it will matter little What we did with our time, but Who we believed in that will make all the difference.

Day 257

Ahhh, Resolutions. It seems that the New Year is the perfect time to make a firm decision to do or not to do something… as if the outcome was completely up to us.

Proverbs 16:9
The heart of man plans his way, but the Lord establishes his steps.

To quote Mike Tyson, "Everyone has a plan until they get punched in the face." Your plans may fail, your resolutions may not last more than a few days, but that's just because God has bigger plans for you. Plans to prosper you and not to harm you, plans to give you hope and a future. (I can't believe I just quoted a man that bit another man's ear off!)

Day 258

As the ball drops in Times Square, we remember a year filled with joys and sorrows, defeats and victories, bitter times and sweet times, our slate is full of memories. But, when it gets to the bottom, in a moment, in the twinkling of an eye, our slate is wiped clean and we begin anew.

2 Corinthians 5:17
Therefore, if anyone is in Christ, he is a new creation. Old things have disappeared, and—look!—all things have become new!

It is truly a mystery. December 31st at 11:59 PM we stand anxiously awaiting the seconds to go by with great expectation and at 12:00 AM, a moment later, we are filled with great excitement and hope. It is the same way the moments before and after we welcome Christ into our heart and make Him our lord and Savior. Happy New Year.

Day 259

I was asked yesterday how to deal with negative thoughts. On doing some research, I was astounded that some 40 million Americans are on medication to deal with negative thoughts. That's one in 5 people! Here are a few verses to explain how you can overcome those thoughts...

Proverbs 29:25
The fear of man brings a snare,
But he who trusts in the Lord will be exalted.

Philippians 4:6
do not be anxious about anything, but in everything by prayer and supplication with thanksgiving let your requests be made known to God.

Ephesians 6
10 Finally, be strong in the Lord and in the strength of His might. 11 Put on the full armor of God, so that you will be able to stand firm against the schemes of the devil. 12 For our struggle is not against flesh and blood, but against the rulers, against the powers, against the world forces of this darkness, against the spiritual forces of wickedness in the heavenly places. 13 Therefore, take up the full armor of God, so that you will be able to resist in the evil day, and having done everything, to stand firm. 14 Stand firm therefore, having girded your loins with truth, and having put on the breastplate of righteousness, 15 and having shod your feet with the preparation of the gospel of peace; 16 in addition to all, taking up the shield of faith with which you will be able to extinguish all the flaming arrows of the evil one. 17 And take the helmet of salvation, and the sword of the Spirit, which is the word of God.

Sorry Gang, that was not a short one but it's a war out there. Read the Bible daily, fill your mind with prayer until there is no room for fear then consume yourself in the joy of the Lord. Arm yourself with the Full Armor of God, then look the enemy in the eyes and shout at the top of your lungs like Rocky Balboa, "I ain't going down no more!"

Day 260

I was once told by a pastor that miracles are problematic because it is too difficult to explain why one person receives the miracle and another person, perhaps just as deserving does not. Answered prayers have strengthened my faith over the years. But what of those prayers that were met with what can only be described as a deafening silence?

Psalm 77:1-20 ESV
I cry aloud to God, aloud to God, and he will hear me. In the day of my trouble I seek the Lord; in the night my hand is stretched out without wearying; my soul refuses to be comforted. When I remember God, I moan; when I meditate, my spirit faints. Selah You hold my eyelids open; I am so troubled that I cannot speak …

I believe we have all cried out to God at one time or another. No matter what the reason may be, when our prayers seemed to fall on deaf ears, it hurt deeply. When a close friend of mine went through a horrific event in his life, his pastor told him with sincerity that he had no idea why some prayers go unanswered and that when he got to heaven, that would be the first thing he would want to ask God. Most impressively, that same pastor, knowing he had no good answers or Bible verses to quote simply asked, "May I sit here with you?" It takes great faith and strength to admit that there are some things we will never be able to explain. I pray that if the time comes, we will have the strength to just sit quietly and comfort those around us whose prayers went unanswered.

Day 261

We have all been faced with the decision when you weren't feeling 100%- Should I go to work/school today or should I just call in and take the day off? The latter sounds better, it makes more sense, it seems like the better choice…Or Is It?

1 Chronicles 28:20
Then David continued, "Be strong and courageous, and do the work. Don't be afraid or discouraged, for the LORD God, my God, is with you. He will not fail you or forsake you. He will see to it that all the work related to the Temple of the LORD is finished correctly."

Listen, there is a time and a place to wave the white flag but in most cases, just suck it up and be strong. Don't be afraid, be courageous. Trust in the Lord. You can do this with His help.

Day 262

Words are important, after all, the world was created with a word. So, when people ask me to "crack" or "manipulate" them or a chiropractor announces that he or she manipulates his or her patients, I CRINGE. The definition of manipulate is to "control or influence (a person or situation) cleverly, unfairly, or unscrupulously." The Bible does not look favorably on that…

Matthew 12:37
For by your words you will be justified, and by your words you will be condemned."

Chiropractors "adjust" their patients, not crack or manipulate. The definition of adjust is to "alter or move (something) slightly in order to achieve the desired fit, appearance, or result; to bring into proper relationship. I love being checked and adjusted but I would never let anyone manipulate me. Words matter. Let's use positive words that encourage and build others up this week and eliminate the negatives. Listen to Aretha's advice… Accentuate the Positives, eliminate the negatives!

Day 263

Oh man, I definitely ate too much this Christmas. We Americans live in the land of the overfed and the undernourished.

Deuteronomy 8:3
He humbled you, causing you to hunger and then feeding you with manna, which neither you nor your ancestors had known, to teach you that man does not live on bread alone but on every word that comes from the mouth of the LORD.

Matthew 4:4
But he answered and said, It is written, Man shall not live by bread alone, but by every word that proceedeth out of the mouth of God.

As many of us sit around with our bellies full, let's remember to give ourselves the nourishment we truly need. Take time to study the Bible each day to fill our spirits or no matter how much we eat, we will still feel empty.

Day 264

Father Joe Upton gave one of the most meaningful Christmas homilies that I have ever heard this morning. Remember Linus from the Charlie Brown comics? Linus, like many of us, carry around a security blanket. The blanket we hold is a FALSE sense of security. In the Charlie Brown Christmas Special, Linus Quotes from Luke 2:8-14. Watch what he does with his blanket when he reads, "do not be afraid" and is liberated from his fear by the message he is sharing...

https://www.youtube.com/watch?v=pn10FF-FQfs (the Linus from the Peanuts Christmas monolog)

In Jesus, we are liberated from fear. We trade our False sense of security for the Real security of knowing that through Him we should "Fear not [there is nothing to fear], for I am with you; do not look around you in terror and be dismayed, for I am your God. I will strengthen and harden you to difficulties, yes, I will help you; yes, I will hold you up and retain you with My [victorious] right hand of rightness and justice." Isaiah 41:10

PS- you're not alone. I never noticed that he dropped his security blanket as he was overcome by the Spirit of God either.

Day 265

Ahhh, Christmas, when the church gets packed by all the Creesters (those that come only on Christmas and Easter). Don't get me wrong, I'm sure they're all well meaning and come intending to start their prayer life anew and create new habits of coming to church more regularly. But, more often than not, the next time we'll find it hard to get a seat in the pews will be Easter...

Luke 2:39-40
39 When they had performed everything according to the Law of the Lord, they returned to Galilee, to their own city of Nazareth. 40 The Child continued to grow and become strong, increasing in wisdom; and the grace of God was upon Him.

Even in the Bible, after Jesus was born, everything went back to normal. They went home and went about their business. Yet, it is in our failure to keep our commitment to God, choosing instead to just "go back to normal", that His Faithfulness is demonstrated to us. For even when we don't show up to church, God shows up to listen to our prayers. Let's keep the Christmas spirit alive this year by Showing Up and listening to God...it's just common courtesy right?

Day 266

A Christmas Eve Reflection

Expectancy. There is perhaps no other night where expectancy is so high as the night when a woman goes into labor. Will it be a boy? Will it be a girl? I can't wait to hold him or her! Imagine the night before Jesus was born. The shepherds were told their Savior will be born tonight by an Angel! Mary and Joseph would finally get to meet God's Son who was entrusted to them!

Luke 2:18-20
18And all who heard it wondered at the things which were told them by the shepherds. 19But Mary treasured all these things, pondering them in her heart. 20The shepherds went back, glorifying and praising God for all that they had heard and seen, just as had been told them.

As kids we couldn't wait to see the presents. Tonight, we as adults, wait with expectancy to see the True Gift be symbolically born again unto us. Merry Christmas, my friends.

Day 267

We have all had unanswered prayers. We have all prayed with great intensity and had prayers answered but those unanswered prayers...what went wrong? Why didn't God grant what we wanted, even begged for?...

Revelation 21:1-5
Then I saw a new heaven and a new earth, for the first heaven and the first earth had passed away, and the sea was no more. And I saw the holy city, new Jerusalem, coming down out of heaven from God, prepared as a bride adorned for her husband. And I heard a loud voice from the throne saying, "Behold, the dwelling place of God is with man. He will dwell with them, and they will be his people, and God himself will be with them as their God. He will wipe away every tear from their eyes, and death shall be no more, neither shall there be mourning, nor crying, nor pain anymore, for the former things have passed away." And he who was seated on the throne said, "Behold, I am making all things new." Also he said, "Write this down, for these words are trustworthy and true."

In God's Time, all our prayers will be answered. All our tears will be wiped away, all pain will be gone and we will dwell with God and our loved ones in a place that makes what we are begging for here on Earth seem unimportant. Keep praying in Faith knowing that the answer to some prayers may take longer to answer than others. Some may have to wait to be fulfilled in New Jerusalem.

Day 268

Ever feel as though your words fell on deaf ears? How would you feel if they fell on a rock?

Luke 8:5-8
5 "The farmer went out to sow his seed; and as he sowed, some fell beside the road, and it was trampled under foot and the birds of the air ate it up. 6 Other seed fell on rocky soil, and as soon as it grew up, it withered away, because it had no moisture. 7 Other seed fell among the thorns; and the thorns grew up with it and choked it out. 8 Other seed fell into the good soil, and grew up, and produced a crop a hundred times as great."

Sometimes your words will be trampled and plucked away by the enemy. Sometimes they will hear your words but forget them quickly. But sometimes, they will hear, through your mouth, the WORD and be transformed forever. Keep spreading the Good News.

Day 269

One of my fondest memories of my Grandma Rose was the delicious Mandel Bread that she made. My wife has carried on the tradition and makes it for me with my grandmother's recipe on my birthday each year. It has become a tradition in our house. The Bible says some traditions are great and some are not so great...

2 Thessalonians 2:15
So then, brothers, stand firm and hold to the traditions that you were taught by us, either by our spoken word or by our letter.

Matthew 15:3
He answered them, "And why do you break the commandment of God for the sake of your tradition?

So, let me set the record straight. Baking my grandma's Mandel Bread is a Good tradition. Some "traditions", addictions and patterns of behavior in our families cause us to break God's commandments, that is Bad. Don't keep doing stuff that's contrary to God's will just because it has been done for generations in your family. In Christ, we are strong enough to become better than those that came before us.

Day 270

Earlier tonight I had a conversation with someone who really enjoys a good game of poker. I was wondering what the Bible had to say about gambling. At first, it appears that the Bible doesn't address this issue until I got into my favorite book of the Bible and some very telling advice…

Proverbs 13:11
Wealth gained hastily will dwindle, but whoever gathers little by little will increase it.

Also a few other timely words from The Word…

1 Timothy 6:9
But those who desire to be rich fall into temptation, into a snare, into many senseless and harmful desires that plunge people into ruin and destruction.

Although gambling may be lawful, it is not helpful in any spiritual way. Any addition or habit that potentially can enslave you should be avoided. Remember you may win Really Big if you gamble but you may lose your soul. Is it really worth it?

Day 271

Birthdays are an important milestone in our lives. Birth and LIFE, well lived in service to God and mankind, are what the Bible is all about. On this day where some of us are celebrating Birth, some of us are mourning a death and some of us are ironically doing both, it is important to remember we should celebrate both LIFE and LIFE Everlasting...

Ecclesiastes 7:1
A good name is better than precious ointment; and the day of death than the day of one's birth.

Now, personally, I don't plan on leaving this life until I am 120. Hey, Moses did it, why not? But, it is good to know that the day of one's death will be even more spectacular than the day of one's birth and we stand before God and Jesus with a great multitude singing Holy, Holy, Holy.

Day 272

The will of God. That's a BIG thought. Ever consider what God's Will for us is?

God's will is "good, pleasing and perfect" (Romans 12:2).

God's will, first and foremost, is that we have a relationship with Him through His Son, Jesus Christ. "This is good, and pleases God our Savior, who wants all men to be saved and to come to a knowledge of the truth" (1 Timothy 2:3-4).

And my favorite…

1 Thessalonians 5:16-18
16 Rejoice always; 17 pray without ceasing; 18 in everything give thanks; for this is God's will for you in Christ Jesus.

Rejoice, Pray, Give Thanks, Have a relationship with God through Jesus. That seems Good, pleasing and perfect to me.

Day 273

After 25 years in practice, I know that stress is the cause of ALL dis-ease in the body. Lord knows that there is plenty of stress to go around these days. Without faith and the comfort of God's promise that through His grace "everything is going to be alright", stress can be overpowering.

Matthew 5:1-48
Seeing the crowds, he went up on the mountain, and when he sat down, his disciples came to him. And he opened his mouth and taught them, saying: "Blessed are the poor in spirit, for theirs is the kingdom of heaven. "Blessed are those who mourn, for they shall be comforted. "Blessed are the meek, for they shall inherit the earth. ...

Psalm 23:4
Even though I walk through the valley of the shadow of death, I will fear no evil, for you are with me; your rod and your staff, they comfort me.

These are verses that I have heard over and over again…but…they are still a comfort to me. The Lord is my rock, my fortress and my deliverer. Doesn't that sound comforting to you? Take a moment to jot down below a verse that has comforted you.

Day 274

Everyone seems so surprised that candidates for President of the United States of America are talking about wars and rumors of wars. Everyone seems so surprised that Muslim radical terrorists and sick attention seeking Americans are targeting and killing Christians. Everyone seems so surprised that teens and young adults are becoming lawless and we are growing numb and cold seeing this all on TV every day or week.

Matthew 24:6-7, 9-12
You will be hearing of wars and rumors of wars. See that you are not frightened, for those things must take place, but that is not yet the end. 7 For nation will rise against nation, and kingdom against kingdom, and in various places there will be famines and earthquakes.
9 "Then they will deliver you to tribulation, and will kill you, and you will be hated by all nations because of My name. 10 At that time many will fall away and will betray one another and hate one another. 11 Many false prophets will arise and will mislead many. 12 Because lawlessness is increased, most people's love will grow cold.

Don't be too surprised, it was predicted almost 2000 years ago in the Bible. Listen, if you haven't asked God to forgive your sins and asked Jesus to become your Lord and Savior I suggest you read Revelation and see what else is predicted. This has been a public service announcement.

Here's an action step for today: Turn off the world news and pick up the Bible. Instead of filling your mind with bad news, fill it today with Good News.

Day 275

I am appalled by the behavior of politicians in both parties these days. We need more public servants and less "leaders". What would a leader look like and sound like if they were leading with biblically sound principles?

Mark 9:34-35
But they kept silent, for on the way they had discussed with one another which of them was the greatest. Sitting down, He called the twelve and said to them, "If anyone wants to be first, he shall be last of all and servant of all."

Mark 10:45 ESV
For even the Son of Man came not to be served but to serve, and to give his life as a ransom for many."

Do we really believe that any one of the politicians we elect to govern our nation would give their life as ransom for many? It's easy to point a finger at these politicians and judge them but are WE serving those that cross our path each day? Are WE willing to be last of all? Would we lay down our life as ransom for many? The way to change the world is to set an example in OUR corner of that world first.

What will we do today to be a better servant? Jot a few ideas down below and strive to act on one of them today.

Day 276

Excuses are like garbage cans. Everyone has one and they all stink. Plus, they're not looked on very well by Jesus...

Luke 14:15-24 (here are a few verses but the whole story is worth the read) ..."Blessed is everyone who will eat bread in the kingdom of God!"... he sent his servant to say to those who had been invited, 'Come, for everything is now ready.' 18 But they all alike began to make excuses. The first said to him, 'I have bought a field, and I must go out and see it. Please have me excused.' 19 And another said, 'I have bought five yoke of oxen, and I go to examine them. Please have me excused.' 20 And another said, 'I have married a wife, and therefore I cannot come.'... 'Go out to the highways and hedges and compel people to come in, that my house may be filled. For I tell you, none of those men who were invited shall taste my banquet.'"

When you're called, don't make any excuses...just show up ready to serve.

Day 277

Ever feel like you are swimming against the current? You're trying to do the right thing but the world seems to be going in the opposite direction. Let's be honest, it looks like those that are enjoying worldly and fleshly pleasures are having a good time. It's enough temptation to make you doubt doing the right thing is really worth it...

1 Corinthians 10:13
No temptation has overtaken you that is not common to man. God is faithful, and he will not let you be tempted beyond your ability, but with the temptation he will also provide the way of escape, that you may be able to endure it.

Matthew 6:19-20
"Do not store up for yourselves treasures on earth, where moth and rust destroy, and where thieves break in and steal." But store up for yourselves treasures in heaven, where neither moth nor rust destroys, and where thieves do not break in or steal;

Do the right thing despite the temptation and doubt the enemy has placed in this world to distract you. Try your best knowing that from time to time you'll fail but taking solace in knowing that we were given God's grace when we accepted Jesus as our savior. Do the right thing. You won't regret it.

Day 278

Do you sing songs to yourself or out loud during the day? Does the joy of the Lord just fill you to the brim and then overflow in the form of song and praise? Turns out, you are not alone. A spirit filled Christian is often a singing Christian...

Colossians 3:16 (NASB)
Let the word of Christ richly dwell within you, with all wisdom teaching and admonishing one another with psalms and hymns and spiritual songs, singing with thankfulness in your hearts to God.

If singing out your praises is not your thing and silence is your way of showing respect to God, that's biblical too. But if you are one of the people that use music to communicate your love for God, don't let anyone dissuade you or silence you. The command to sing is simple. Sing to God with gratitude in your hearts!

What song inspires you? Go listen to it now and "Get it stuck in your head" today.

Day 279

What Child is this? None other than the sinless, supernatural Savior "who was conceived by the Holy Ghost, born of the Virgin Mary; suffered under Pontius Pilate, was crucified, dead, and buried . . . the third day He rose again from the dead; He ascended into heaven, and is seated on the right hand of God the Father Almighty; from thence He shall come to judge the living and the dead."

Luke 2:7 ESV
And she gave birth to her firstborn son and wrapped him in swaddling cloths and laid him in a manger, because there was no place for them in the inn.

Where would you expect the King of Kings to be born…in a castle right? Instead God chose a smelly manger. Though he was rich, yet for your sake he became poor, so that by his poverty he could make you rich. THAT is a lot to think about…

Write down YOUR definition of being rich below.

Day 280

Immanuel means —"God with us". Ever really think about that... what it took for God to be fully God and human at the same time?

"In the beginning was the Word, and the Word was with God, and the Word was God. . . . The Word became flesh and made his dwelling among us. We have seen his glory, the glory of the One and Only, who came from the Father, full of grace and truth" (John 1:1, 14).

So, let's try to wrap our heads around this. God left Heaven to become fully human, because He could not bear the thought of you spending an eternity in Hell. "As in Adam all die, so in Christ all will be made alive" (1 Corinthians 15:22). And yet you wonder if God loves you? Really?

Reflect on the depth of Gods love for you today not through what He's given you but for what He has given for you.

Day 281

Many of us have, or know someone who has, physical or spiritual "pain". It may have just started recently or it might be something that has lingered on for years. Either way pain is a terrible thing. Now what I am about to say is really tough to take at first...Pain can have some benefits..

Romans 5:3-4 ESV
More than that, we rejoice in our sufferings, knowing that suffering produces endurance, and endurance produces character, and character produces hope,

Rejoice in Suffering?? That sounds crazy! But when you think about it, it was in the times we were in the most pain that we were brought to our knees and it was there that we were closest to God. It is on our knees that we can most sincerely ask for forgiveness of our sins, redemption, love, mercy and even healing.

Psalm 103:2-4 ESV
Bless the Lord, O my soul, and forget not all his benefits, who forgives all your iniquity, who heals all your diseases, who redeems your life from the pit, who crowns you with steadfast love and mercy,

Day 282

Ever felt like you just needed to vent and were glad a friend was there to listen? Now let's turn the tables. Last time a friend of yours needed to vent, did you listen intently and give them compassion and wise counsel?

James 1:19-20 ESV
Know this, my beloved brothers: let every person be quick to hear, slow to speak, slow to anger; for the anger of man does not produce the righteousness of God.

1 Peter 3:15 ESV
But in your hearts honor Christ the Lord as holy, always being prepared to make a defense to anyone who asks you for a reason for the hope that is in you; yet do it with gentleness and respect,

God gave us two ears and one mouth for a reason. Be the person who is quick to hear and then gently offers a reason not to lose hope.

Who can you think of that needs to be listened to more? Maybe it's a person that you have been taking for granted that is always there to listen to you but you haven't given them enough time to talk while you listen.

Day 283

When someone is going through a rough time, we often pray for them to experience a sense of peace. That peace has been given to us by God through the Holy Spirit...

Philippians 4:6-7
Don't worry about anything; instead, pray about everything. Tell God what you need, and thank him for all he has done. Then you will experience God's peace, which exceeds anything we can understand. His peace will guard your hearts and minds as you live in Christ Jesus.

Peace be with you.

Take a moment to write down the names of the people you most desire for God to grant peace to and then pray for them right now.

Day 284

I love Saturday night and Sunday because I get to spend time in worship to God and praise Him with my wife. Do you know what my Favorite day of the week is? Monday is my favorite day!

James 2:14-26
14 What does it profit, my brethren, if someone says he has faith but does not have works? Can faith save him?...
18 But someone will say, "You have faith, and I have works." Show me your faith without your[a] works, and I will show you my faith by my[b] works...
22 Do you see that faith was working together with his works, and by works faith was made perfect?...
26 For as the body without the spirit is dead, so faith without works is dead also.

I gave you the Cliff notes version above, the whole thing is worth a read but the point is that we can sing and worship all we want on Sunday but if we don't put our faith to work on Monday, we don't really "Get The BIG Idea". Faith creates the works and our works Complete our faith. So, what are you waiting for? GET TO WORK ☺:) !

What will you do today as a work to express your faith?

Day 285

I was inspired by a story that Father Jared shared during his homily about a young man that finds his way to St. Patrick's Cathedral in NYC. People are streaming in and out around him and the priest notices that he looks distressed so the priest decides to approach him and ask if everything is alright. The young man says, "No. I feel like I have lost God." The priest asks, "Where did you lose Him?" The young man points to his heart and says, "In here." The priest then advises him, "Then search your heart and that is where you will find Him again."

Jeremiah 29:13
You will seek me and find me, when you seek me with all your heart.

Have you ever felt like you've lost God? Have you wandered so far from Him that you don't know if you can find your way back to Him? He's right where you left him…In your heart.

Today, examine your heart. Search it thoroughly. Write below what you found if you can describe it with words.

Day 286

Have you seen the front page newspaper article that scythes people for saying their thoughts and prayers are with the victim's families because the author is appalled that God did not intervene and prevent the shooting? As believers it's OK to ask, "If God has the power to eradicate evil and suffering, then why doesn't He do it?"

2 Peter 3:9
"The Lord is not slow in keeping His promise, as some understand slowness. He is patient with you, not wanting anyone to perish, but everyone to come to repentance."

The day will come when sickness and pain will be eradicated and people will be held accountable for the evil they've committed. Justice will be served in a perfect way. That day will come, but not yet. He's actually delaying the consummation of history in anticipation that some of you will still put your trust in Him and spend eternity in heaven. That's evidence of a loving God, that He would care that much for you and those you love.

Take some time to write down things below that you have observed in your life which demonstrates evidence of a loving God.

Day 287

Does practice REALLY make perfect?...

Ecclesiastes 7:20
Surely there is not a righteous man on earth who does good and never sins.

Matthew 5:48
You therefore must be perfect, as your heavenly Father is perfect.

Practice doesn't make perfect. Perfect Practice makes perfect. Since we can not be perfect and we will all fall to sin in our fleshly bodies, we can only become perfect IN God and Through Jesus. How can we practice becoming more like Jesus? Keep reading the Truth.

Open your Bible and just read for a minute or two then write about what God spoke to you about through the Word in just a few sentences.

Day 288

I had a good friend ask if the Holy Spirit "runs" our body. That's a great question because even though it dwells within us, and does have a lot to do with a body, its not necessarily what you may think at first…

1 Corinthians 6:19
Or do you not know that your body is a temple of the Holy Spirit within you, whom you have from God? You are not your own,

1 Corinthians 12:13
For in one Spirit we were all baptized into one body—Jews or Greeks, slaves or free—and all were made to drink of one Spirit.

We run our body, that is what free will is but we are called through our faith to keep it clean because it is the temple of God where the Holy Spirit dwells. However, we are grafted into the body that will count for eternity, the Body of Christ, through our baptism when the Holy Spirit descends upon us and takes residence in the depths of our earthly body.

What do you do to "keep your body clean" on a daily basis?

Day 289

If you want more happiness, do more things to make others happy. If you want more love, love others more deeply. If you want more money, tithe more. Whatever it is you need, give more of it away.

Malachi 3:10
Bring the full tithe into the storehouse, that there may be food in my house. And thereby put me to the test, says the Lord of hosts, if I will not open the windows of heaven for you and pour down for you a blessing until there is no more need.

Proverbs 11:24
One gives freely, yet grows all the richer; another withholds what he should give, and only suffers want.

This is the only place in the Bible when God dares you to test Him, in all other places it is a sin. When it comes to Tithing, giving cheerfully is paid back with abundance. Give freely and you'll become abundant in that which you give. Withhold that which you desperately need because you think you have so little of it and you'll never have enough.

What will you give away today?

Day 290

So, what is this Advent season? It's not mentioned in the Bible so should we observe it? What is it anyway? That is a question that I had as I explored my faith. Here is what I found:

Psalm 62:5-7
For God alone my soul waits in silence,
for my hope is from him.
He alone is my rock and my salvation,
my fortress; I shall not be shaken.

Romans 8:24-25
For in hope we have been saved, but hope that is seen is not hope; for who hopes for what he already sees? But if we hope for what we do not see, with perseverance we wait eagerly for it.

You can't turn to a place in the Bible and find a teaching on Advent or a command to set aside four weeks prior to Christmas as a season of waiting, hoping, and yearning. Having said that, if it helps you to prepare yourself for the coming of Jesus Christ by renewing your hope in silent prayer awaiting the jubilation of His birth…then Go For It!

Let's not wait until Advent to prepare our heart for the coming of Jesus. Write down one thing that you'll do this week to prepare your heart.

Day 291

Money is no longer people's most valued commodity. In today's stressful, hustle and bustle life, we are working harder and longer than ever. We have become taxi drivers for our overscheduled kids' lives, we go from appointment to appointment, there never seems to be a time to stop and smell the roses…

1 Corinthians 10:31
So, whether you eat or drink, or whatever you do, do everything for the glory of God.

Another Bible verse tells us that where we put our treasure, so lies our heart. The enemy will tempt us with un-Godly things to do with our new treasure, our time. Today, maybe we should examine how we're spending our time and if what we're doing during that time is being done for the glory of God.

Think about your day. Where are you spending the bulk of each day? Where are you spending the bulk of each week? What are you doing during the bulk of your free time? Take a minute and write down a new plan for your free time below.

Day 292

It's easy to dole out judgement and get caught up in gossip in today's society, Sometimes we're even pretty tough on our pastors and teachers.

1 Corinthians 4:1-6
So look at Apollos and me as mere servants of Christ who have been put in charge of explaining God's mysteries. Now, a person who is put in charge as a manager must be faithful. As for me, it matters very little how I might be evaluated by you or by any human authority. I don't even trust my own judgment on this point. My conscience is clear, but that doesn't prove I'm right. It is the Lord himself who will examine me and decide.

So maybe we should dole out less judgment and begin looking for reasons to Praise those we care about and people that care about us. Our time of judgment grows nearer with each breath and He will bring our darkest secrets to light and will reveal our private motives. If that day were today, what would He praise you for? Take a moment and write those things down below.

Day 293

Black Friday

Today is Black Friday. Not the best holiday if you are trying to get closer to your Maker. Do we really need all this STUFF? I mean, what's really important?

Matthew 6:19-21
"Do not lay up for yourselves treasures on earth, where moth and rust destroy and where thieves break in and steal, but lay up for yourselves treasures in heaven, where neither moth nor rust destroys and where thieves do not break in and steal. For where your treasure is, there your heart will be also.

Don't be attached to material things. Black is the absence of color. Darkness is the absence of light. Instead of celebrating black Friday, how about we focus on the Light of the World, on The Lord God Almighty, the Source of Life and Abundance and Treasure beyond our wildest imagination.

Take the space below and write down anything you can buy on Black Friday that's more important than God. Go ahead, there's plenty of room…

Day 294

Happy Thanksgiving! Today is the day the Lord has made, let us rejoice and be glad in it!

Psalm 100:1-5
A Psalm for giving thanks. Make a joyful noise to the Lord, all the earth! Serve the Lord with gladness! Come into his presence with singing! Know that the Lord, he is God! It is he who made us, and we are his; we are his people, and the sheep of his pasture. Enter his gates with thanksgiving, and his courts with praise! Give thanks to him; bless his name! For the Lord is good; his steadfast love endures forever, and his faithfulness to all generations.

When is the last time you received a hand written thank you note in the mail? How did that make you feel? That is sort of what prayers of thanksgiving and praise are to God.

Take a minute to actually hand write a thank you note to someone you care about today.

Day 295

You ever notice that you can't spell "integrity" without using the word "grit"? Well, you can't have integrity in your life without it either. Just ask Job.

Job 2:7-10
Satan left the LORD's presence, and he struck Job with terrible boils from head to foot.
Job scraped his skin with a piece of broken pottery as he sat among the ashes. His wife said to him, "Are you still trying to maintain your integrity? Curse God and die."
But Job replied, "You talk like a foolish woman. Should we accept only good things from the hand of God and never anything bad?" So in all this, Job said nothing wrong.

Integrity means doing the right thing even when everyone else is going wrong. And it's rarely easy. But it's worth it. Ask God for the strength to have integrity today.

Let's pray together. Lord God, with all the craziness going on in the world, give me the strength to be a light in the darkness. Please give me the ability to be honest in a world of lies and have integrity when others around me do not.

Day 296

There's something very special about early morning prayer. The body is well rested, the world is still and the mind is quiet. Many people tell me they have a hard time hearing God speak to them. I wonder if they have consistently woken early to pray and listen…

Proverbs 8:17
I love those who love me, and those who seek me diligently find me.

Mark 1:35
And rising very early in the morning, while it was still dark, he departed and went out to a desolate place, and there he prayed.

Early to bed, Early to rise… (you know the rest)

What time will you set your alarm clock for tomorrow morning?

Day 297

I get a kick out of people who believe in Coincidences. They are actually God-Incidences. You find $5 and a homeless guy asks you for money... You are thinking about someone you care about and the phone rings for you to discover it is them... You wake to the sound of a Tornado, you grab the kids with your wife and without having time to get to the basement you just happen to huddle above the kids in one of the only parts of the house that was safe (yeah, that really happened to us)...

Romans 8:28 And we know that for those who love God all things work together for good, for those who are called according to his purpose.

Satan tries to discourage us by making us think it was just a coincidence. Tell Satan he's a liar. Let him know that YOU KNOW it was the mighty hand of God and He will never forsake me. Coincidences are how faithless people explain away miracles.

What coincidences in your life, looking back now, may have actually been the hand of God working in your life? Jot a few down here:

Day 298

There are lots of temptations and distractions in our world today. They draw us away from what is truly important like our spouse, our children, our family, our calling in life and our faith.

1 Corinthians 10:13
No temptation has overtaken you that is not common to man. God is faithful, and he will not let you be tempted beyond your ability, but with the temptation he will also provide the way of escape, that you may be able to endure it.

Whether it is Facebook, the internet, food, your "smart" phone, or whatever appears greener on the other side of the fence, know that God has placed within you the ability to overcome its temptation. Focus on eliminating the distractions and begin spending time regaining balance in your life Today.

What's one distraction you can write down here on this page that you can commit to eliminating today?

Day 299

Procrastination seems like the easiest thing to do. We're all guilty of if from time to time. God calls us to get the job done now, not later.

Proverbs 3:27-28
Do not withhold good from those to whom it is due,
When it is in your power to do it.
Do not say to your neighbor, "Go, and come back,
And tomorrow I will give it,"
When you have it with you.

What have we been putting off that we can get done today?

Write it here and commit to getting it done in the next 30 days.

Day 300

Finding your calling in life can be difficult. I realized why God put me on Earth at a very young age. For some it can be a life long search for your calling. God promises us that just as a body has many parts and each has a special purpose, he has created us with a special talent and purpose. Once you have found your calling, here's some important advice from the Truth…

Ephesians 4:1-3 I therefore, a prisoner for the Lord, urge you to walk in a manner worthy of the calling to which you have been called, with all humility and gentleness, with patience, bearing with one another in love, eager to maintain the unity of the Spirit in the bond of peace.

Demonstrate to the world what it is like to be filled with the Holy Spirit while you are at work by walking uprightly, being humble, being gentle, having patience and loving generously. Although the search for your calling may not be easy, it is worthwhile. When you find your calling, your work will become your play and your play will become your work and you will never have to work again.

If you could do anything in the world and you knew you couldn't fail, what would you do? Write it down here.

Day 301

In our lives, we have all been led astray. We have wandered away from "home" searching for "something better". Sometimes "home" was our parents, sometimes it was our faith, and sometimes it was our morals, principles or even our health. The story of Jacob in the Old Testament (Genesis 35) teaches us about this lesson but there is perhaps no story in the Bible easier to relate to than that of the Prodigal Son.

Luke 15:11-32
...the younger son gathered everything together and went on a journey into a distant country, and there he squandered his estate with loose living. ... 17 But when he came to his senses he said ... "Father, I have sinned against heaven, and in your sight; 19 I am no longer worthy to be called your son; make me as one of your hired men."... 20 So he got up and came to his father. But while he was still a long way off, his father saw him and felt compassion for him, and ran and embraced him and kissed him... 24 for this son of mine was dead and has come to life again; he was lost and has been found.' And they began to celebrate.

We have all wondered far from "home" but it is comforting to know it is never too late to make things right and return to God's warm embrace. He has been waiting for you all this time and going home is as easy as bowing your head and speaking to him through prayer right now.

What have you wandered away from in your life in search of something better?

Day 302

Immutability. It's the opposite of mutate. In fact, God is immutable. That means God does not change. Not a smidgen, not at all. He is, has been, and always will be the same.

Malachi 3:6:
"I am the LORD, and I do not change."

If you've ever been in a relationship that fell apart because you or the other person changed, you can appreciate this characteristic about God. He has always been good and holy and he always will be. His love and justice are as solid as a rock. You can never completely understand God, but you can trust character will never change.

What principles do you stand on and never waiver on? What do you find so important in life that you are unwilling to ever entertain the notion of changing? Write some of your thoughts here:

Day 303

Ever been in this conversation? "So, where do you want to go eat tonight?" "You pick, I don't care." "I'm good with whatever." "Food. I want food for dinner." "Argh!" The bad news is we tend to pray like that... "Tell me your needs." "I want to serve more people, Lord. But only if it's your will." "You've blessed me with so much already. I can't ask for anything else."

Matthew 7:7-11
"Keep on asking, and you will receive what you ask for. Keep on seeking, and you will find. Keep on knocking, and the door will be opened to you. For everyone who asks, receives. Everyone who seeks, finds. And to everyone who knocks, the door will be opened. --- "So if you sinful people know how to give good gifts to your children, how much more will your heavenly Father give good gifts to those who ask him."

Ok, none of those prayers are wrong, per se, but they miss the point that God is a gracious and a giving God. God may still say "no," for reasons that are bigger than our ability to comprehend, but how will you know until you boldly ask?

What will you boldly ask for in prayer today?

Day 304

I have people I serve in the office that literally work 7 days a week. The 60% of Americans that are actually working, have somehow been goaded into working our lives away…sometimes to achieve wealth that will never amount to much…sometimes just to make ends meet. Often we are verbally attacked by stressed out people when we take a week or even a day off because they themselves have not understood these words from the Truth…

Mark 6:31
And he said to them, "Come away by yourselves to a desolate place and rest a while." For many were coming and going, and they had no leisure even to eat.

Heberews 4:9-11
So then, there remains a Sabbath rest for the people of God, for whoever has entered God's rest has also rested from his works as God did from his. Let us therefore strive to enter that rest, so that no one may fall by the same sort of disobedience.

So, we are encouraged by God to take vacations to rest in desolate places where there is no cell phone signal or TV reception as well as taking one day a week to rest, worship Him and keep the Sabbath holy. Work hard, Play hard, Rest often…

Have you planned your next vacation or stay-cation? Take time to plan it today.

Day 305

If you have been trying to make an important decision lately, it is important to go to God in prayer and listen carefully. Part of getting the right answer is about getting the Ego out of the way and not make your decision considering how it will effect just you but also how it will effect those around you...

Philippians 2:1-10 So if there is any encouragement in Christ, any comfort from love, any participation in the Spirit, any affection and sympathy, complete my joy by being of the same mind, having the same love, being in full accord and of one mind. Do nothing from rivalry or conceit, but in humility count others more significant than yourselves. Let each of you look not only to his own interests, but also to the interests of others. Have this mind among yourselves, which is yours in Christ Jesus, ...

It is tough to get rid of the ego! Try this prayer... "God, please empty me of me and fill me with you. Empty me Lord of me, Fill me with you." See how you feel after praying that for a while.

Have you been putting off an important decision? Pray on it today and make that decision.

Day 306

I was asked what I do about people that are like sandpaper…you know the type…they are abrasive and rub you the wrong way. Sometimes they rub you so raw that it hurts. What are we called to do? You may not like the answer…

Ephesians 4:1-3
I therefore, a prisoner for the Lord, urge you to walk in a manner worthy of the calling to which you have been called, with all humility and gentleness, with patience, bearing with one another in love, eager to maintain the unity of the Spirit in the bond of peace.

Proverbs 12:16
The vexation of a fool is known at once, but the prudent ignores an insult.

Matthew 5:40
And if anyone would sue you and take your tunic, let him have your cloak as well.

So, the answer is to Have Patience, Love them, ignore their insults and if they take your stuff, offer them the rest of it to take as well. That is one tall order! Reading that is tough, typing it was harder but doing it will take becoming more like Jesus and a lot more prayer.

What will you do when confronted by an abrasive person today?

Day 307

I have been waking very early in the morning spending much more time in preparation for my day recently. My days have seemed to be more blessed as a result of it…

Proverbs 6:6-8
Go to the ant, O sluggard; consider her ways, and be wise. Without having any chief, officer, or ruler, she prepares her bread in summer and gathers her food in harvest.

Interesting that some adults have not learned anything from the fable of the ants and the grasshopper. Be an ant today, don't be a grasshopper…

If you've never read Aesop's fable about the ants and the grasshopper, take the time to do that now.

Day 308

You shouldn't hoot with the owls at night if you want to soar with the eagles in the morning!

Mark 1:35
And rising very early in the morning, while it was still dark, he departed and went out to a desolate place, and there he prayed.

Psalm 119:148
My eyes are awake before the watches of the night, that I may meditate on your promise.

Psalm 143:8
Let me hear in the morning of your steadfast love, for in you I trust. Make me know the way I should go, for to you I lift up my soul.

Wow, 5 AM comes early in the morning when you go to bed at 11:45 at night but waking early seems to be biblical...

How about setting your alarm clock an hour earlier tomorrow morning and read the Bible for a while?

Day 309

OK, day one of waking up at 5 AM to regain my health. Was just wondering what the Bible says about beginning a journey as I type while walking at 4 miles per hour (which seems to be the fastest I can walk and type at the same time).

Jeremiah 29:11
For I know the plans I have for you, declares the Lord, plans for welfare and not for evil, to give you a future and a hope.

Ephesians 4:22-24
To put off your old self, which belongs to your former manner of life and is corrupt through deceitful desires, and to be renewed in the spirit of your minds, and to put on the new self, created after the likeness of God in true righteousness and holiness.

May God bless you today and any new journey you are embarking on and thanks to my good friend Rob who texted me this morning to make sure I was up and ready to work out! Its time to kick this treadmill up to 5 before I pick up the weights.

What important goal have you been putting off? Write it down here and do whatever it takes to accomplish it tomorrow.

Day 310

When you're down and troubled
and you need a helping hand,
and nothing, whoa nothing is going right.
Close your eyes and think of me
And soon i will be there
to brighten up even your darkest nights.

Ecclesiastes 4:9-10
Two are better than one, because they have a good reward for their toil. For
if they fall, one will lift up his fellow. But woe to him who is alone when he
falls and has not another to lift him up!
Luckily, as Christians, we always have a friend to pick us up when we are
down. His name is Jesus....

You just call out my name,
and you know wherever I am
I'll come running, oh yeah baby
to see you again.
Winter, spring, summer, or fall,
all you got to do is call
and I'll be there, yeah, yeah, yeah.
You've got a friend.

Write the names of your most cherished friends here and then contact them
today to let them know how much you appreciate them.

Day 311

Discipline is not a joy ride. Just like the Israelites, we all get reprimanded by the Lord. It's not fun, but it grows our trust and reliance on him.

Deuteronomy 8:2-5
Remember how the LORD your God led you through the wilderness for these forty years, humbling you and testing you to prove your character, and to find out whether or not you would obey his commands. Yes, he humbled you by letting you go hungry and then feeding you with manna, a food previously unknown to you and your ancestors. He did it to teach you that people do not live by bread alone; rather, we live by every word that comes from the mouth of the LORD. For all these forty years your clothes didn't wear out, and your feet didn't blister or swell. Think about it: Just as a parent disciplines a child, the LORD your God disciplines you for your own good.

Keep in mind, his loving discipline only lasts a little while. But his goodness, it lasts forever!

Can you think of a time when you were disciplined that helped you later in life? Write a few thoughts about it here:

Day 312

So, my favorite baseball team made it to the World Series but last night the Mets lost to the Royals. There must be a lesson in there somewhere...

Philippians 2:3
Do nothing from rivalry or conceit, but in humility count others more significant than yourselves.

1 Corinthisans 9:25
Every athlete exercises self-control in all things. They do it to receive a perishable wreath, but we an imperishable.

So, as it turns out there are two lessons here. Be a good sport and give credit where credit is due. AND, we may win prizes here on Earth from time to time but the real prize is our faith which gives us the imperishable prize of eternity with our Creator.

What lessons can be learned in being a good loser and in being a gracious winner?

Day 313

Set The Clock Back Day

So, did you remember to set your clock back an hour last night? Pretty sweet to have an extra hour to rest, huh? If you think that's cool, take a look at what God did with time when one of his servants cried out in prayer for help...

Joshua 10:12-14
12 At that time Joshua spoke to the LORD in the day when the LORD gave the Amorites over to the sons of Israel, and he said in the sight of Israel, "Sun, stand still at Gibeon,
and moon, in the Valley of Aijalon."
13 And the sun stood still, and the moon stopped,
until the nation took vengeance on their enemies.
Is this not written in the Book of Jashar? The sun stopped in the midst of heaven and did not hurry to set for about a whole day. 14 There has been no day like it before or since, when the LORD heeded the voice of a man, for the LORD fought for Israel.

God didn't just set the clocks back an hour. He halted the movement of the sun and the moon for about 24 hours in response to a prayer from a faithful servant. Have you prayed today?

If you could turn back time and do one thing differently, what would that be?

Day 314

So great! You've decided to follow Jesus. All that's left is to learn how you're supposed to live...for the rest of your life.

Here's a little help from Ephesians 4:29-32:
Don't use foul or abusive language. Let everything you say be good and helpful, so that your words will be an encouragement to those who hear them.
And do not bring sorrow to God's Holy Spirit by the way you live. Remember, he has identified you as his own, guaranteeing that you will be saved on the day of redemption. Get rid of all bitterness, rage, anger, harsh words, and slander, as well as all types of evil behavior. Instead, be kind to each other, tenderhearted, forgiving one another, just as God through Christ has forgiven you

When it's all said and done, it comes down to this: God gives us the power to become more like Jesus. That process isn't always easy, but you'll find that the changes in your life and relationships will be worth it.

What's one way you can become more like Jesus today?

Day 315

Electricity is an interesting thing. When used properly it can add light to dark places and be used to warm our homes. If it is used carelessly, it can kill you. Words are like electricity...

Proverbs 18:21
The tongue can bring death or life; those who love to talk will reap the consequences.

Matt 12:36
I tell you, on the day of judgment people will give account for every careless word they speak,

When given the choice today, will you speak Life and Blessings over those you encounter? Or, will you say something you may regret and reap the consequences? Choose your words wisely today. Whether you are talking to yourself or someone else, I'm confident God is rooting for you to choose words that are a blessing to his children.

Write down one way that you can be a blessing to someone else today. (Then go do it!)

Day 316

Did you see the crowds the Pope attracted in his "Pope-mobile"? Well years ago, when Jesus was on his way to Jericho, the crowds were even bigger. As Jesus passed Bartimaeus, a blind beggar, Bartimaeus began to shout, "Jesus, Son of David, have mercy on me." He shouted it over and over again. The crowd got agitated and told him to shut up. He was ruining the moment screaming as the "Jesus-mobile" went by. Jesus didn't think he was ruining the moment though, stopped the procession and called him over to ask a question…

Luke 18:41-42
"What do you want me to do for you?" "Lord, I want to see," he replied. Jesus said to him, "Receive your sight; your faith has healed you."

"What can I do to help you?" Aren't those the words we long to hear when we are in need and hurting? Jesus asks us this question each time we cry out to Him. More importantly, just as he works in us, He works through us. Next time we are confronted by the blind beggar, will we lead him to the front of the crowd to meet Jesus or push him to the back and tell him to shut up? Are we blind or has our faith healed us?

Jesus is asking us today, "What can I do to help you?" What is your response? Write it here as though it were a letter to Him.

Day 317

Have you ever wondered who and what the Holy Spirit is for?

1 John 4:13-15
And God has given us his Spirit as proof that we live in him and he in us.
Furthermore, we have seen with our own eyes and now testify that the
Father sent his Son to be the Savior of the world. All who confess that Jesus
is the Son of God have God living in them, and they live in God.

So one of the reasons you have the Holy Spirit is proof that you belong to
God...and now, it's our responsibility to tell other people about it. God
doesn't have to be "sold" to anyone, He only needs to be introduced to the
person who needs Him.

Who will you introduce to God today?

Day 318

If you end up watching paint dry today, water boil or grass grow and are bored, here is something Biblical to do..

1 Thes 5...
16 Rejoice always; 17 pray without ceasing; 18 in everything give thanks

I'll bet that's the shortest devotional page but...
That ought to keep us busy today...

Day 319

One of my favorite TV pastors was Robert H. Schuller. He taught me a long time ago that "Tough times never last, but tough people do!"

James 1:2-4
Count it all joy, my brothers, when you meet trials of various kinds, for you know that the testing of your faith produces steadfastness. And let steadfastness have its full effect, that you may be perfect and complete, lacking in nothing.

There are dozens of verses about how God promises to help us through tough times. The bottom line is that whatever you are facing today is only temporary. Life is a marathon, not a sprint. Run the whole race knowing that even if you feel a little behind right now, if you continue to run in faith, God will be waiting for you at the finish line with open arms and the words, "Well done, my good and faithful servant."

Are you facing an adversity in your life right now? Take the time now to pray to God and ask Him for His guidance, His peace and His divine help.

Day 320

I once heard a story of a man trying to cut down a tree with a dull saw. His friend saw him and suggested that he Stop, take time to sharpen the saw and Rest for a while. To this, the man replied, "I would but I don't have enough time. Can't you see I'm too busy trying to cut down this tree to take any time to sharpen my saw or Rest?"

Matthew 11:28-30
Come to me, all who labor and are heavy laden, and I will give you rest. Take my yoke upon you, and learn from me, for I am gentle and lowly in heart, and you will find rest for your souls. For my yoke is easy, and my burden is light."

Mark 6:31
And he said to them, "Come away by yourselves to a desolate place and rest a while." For many were coming and going, and they had no leisure even to eat.

Have you taken time to sharpen your saw and rest lately? Admitting you have a problem is the first step to getting help. Have you taken the time to rest lately? If not, schedule it with yourself right here and right now.

Day 321

The way of the world is to look out for yourself--do what you want. They think, "If I can do it, and I want to, I should." Paul talks about reversing the system.

1 Corinthians 10:23-24
You say, "I am allowed to do anything"--but not everything is good for you.
You say, "I am allowed to do anything"--but not everything is beneficial.

Don't be concerned for your own good but for the good of others.
Looking out for others first, reverses the game.

Write down one kind deed you can do for someone else today:

Day 322

Ever been in pain? Occasionally we are reminded that we are human and we experience pain in this life. Sometimes it is physical, sometimes it is psychological but we must focus on the promise that God will get us through it…

Rev 21:4
and He will wipe away every tear from their eyes; and there will no longer be any death; there will no longer be any mourning, or crying, or pain; the first things have passed away."

Any way you slice it, it sucks to be in pain. The worst part of pain is when you are right in the middle of it and there seems that there is nothing to do about it and it seems as though it will never end. In that time, draw nearer to God. Focus on the fact that He is with you in that moment and He promises a time that there will no longer be any pain.

What can you do to ease your suffering or someone you care about's suffering?

Day 323

The passage of the rich young man was read in church this weekend. It struck me how much we are held in bondage by all our "stuff". You don't need to have a Ferrari or a mansion to be possessed by your possessions. Even the homeless person will fight to keep what is in his/her shopping cart....Why?

Mathew 19:20-22
20 The young man *said to Him, "All these things I have kept; what am I still lacking?" 21 Jesus said to him, "If you wish to be [a]complete, go and sell your possessions and give to the poor, and you will have treasure in heaven; and come, follow Me." 22 But when the young man heard this statement, he went away grieving; for he was one who owned much property.

Stop for a minute today and consider what is really valuable in your life. When we die, we will all leave exactly the same amount of stuff...all of it. Where does your treasure lie?

Day 324

Hey, you going through some stuff today? The apostle Paul was in prison, yet he knew inner peace. So how do you get that?

Philippians 4:6-7
Don't worry about anything; instead, pray about everything. Tell God what you need, and thank him for all he has done. Then you will experience God's peace, which exceeds anything we can understand. His peace will guard your hearts and minds as you live in Christ Jesus.

Look, God's peace can guard your heart against hurt and pain. But that only happens if you take your problems to God. Worry less, pray more. Look to the past and be thankful for what God has already done.

What do you have to be grateful for today? Don't cop out. Answer the question. Sometimes the littlest things are the most precious. Write some things down here:

Day 325

Hey, it's okay to be tired. That's normal. Just be careful where you turn for strength.

Isaiah 40:30-31
Even youths will become weak and tired,
and young men will fall in exhaustion.
But those who trust in the Lord will find new strength.
They will soar high on wings like eagles.
They will run and not grow weary.
They will walk and not faint.

Trust the Lord. That's where your strength is.

List some of your strengths here:

Day 326

There are 4 words for love, 3 are used in the Bible. They are agape, phileo, storge, and eros. Eros is the sexual type of love that is not found in the Bible. Storge is a brotherly kind of love found in Romans 12:10. Phileo is the type of love we have for a close friend. Agape is the unconditional love of God and is the love shown through obedience and commitment by His children to Him.

The difference between agape and phileo becomes very clear in John 21:15. After being raised from the dead, Jesus met Peter. Here is the short version of what they said to each other.

Jesus: Simon…do you love (agape) me more than these [fish?].
Peter: Yes, Lord; you know that I love (phileo) you.
Jesus: Simon…do you…love (agape) me?
Peter: Yes, Lord, you know that I love (phileo) you.
Jesus: Simon…do you love (agape) me?
Peter: [Grieved] "Lord…you know that I love (phileo) you."

Imagine Peter's grief and sorrow after having denied Jesus 3 times and he must admit to the risen Messiah that he did not Agape Jesus after Jesus died on the cross for him. Jesus Agape loves us and proved it on the cross.

Search your soul…Do you love (agape) Him?

Day 327

You know, millions of dollars, power, penthouse suites, maybe a servant or two, a private party on the yacht... Sounds enticing?

Proverbs 16:8
Better to have little, with godliness,
than to be rich and dishonest.

No matter how appealing all that stuff is, remember that God demands truth. Do you know how much of all the stuff you have collected and the money you have saved that you will leave when you die? All of it.

What treasures have you saved up in Heaven?

Day 328

We all choose our attitudes. Today, choose to rejoice! It's your option.

Philippians 4:4-5
Always be full of joy in the Lord. I say it again--rejoice! Let everyone see that you are considerate in all you do. Remember, the Lord is coming soon.

Christ may not come back to earth today, but through your joyful attitude, he may come into someone else's life!

Write down some of the things you are joyful for in your life...

Day 329

Worry, doubt, bitterness--it's easy to get caught up in feelings like these. But we don't have to!

Psalm 91:14-15
The LORD says, "I will rescue those who love me.
I will protect those who trust in my name.
When they call on me, I will answer;
I will be with them in trouble.
I will rescue and honor them."

No matter what the problem is, these are your answers--love, trust, pray.

Who will you tell you love today? Who will you trust today? Who will you pray for today?

Day 330

We get caught up in life sometimes. And then the commute, the workload or the homework all start to feel like chores. We get mad because someone drives too slowly; we get frustrated because we have work to do. But, sometimes, we just need to stop and think about how good life is, how much we have, and what we're really called here to do.

1 Thessalonians 5:14-18
Brothers and sisters, we urge you to warn those who are lazy. Encourage those who are timid. Take tender care of those who are weak. Be patient with everyone.
See that no one pays back evil for evil, but always try to do good to each other and to all people.
Always be joyful. Never stop praying. Be thankful in all circumstances, for this is God's will for you who belong to Christ Jesus.

We are blessed, and sometimes we take that for granted. It's time to raise the bar. With good and joyfulness and prayer and thanks. Raise that bar and start living.

Let's count our blessings today. What blessings are you most grateful for?

Day 331

You ever feel like you don't have much to give God? Never fear! Jesus says that's actually the way it's supposed to be.

Luke 13:18-19
Then Jesus said, "What is the Kingdom of God like? How can I illustrate it? It is like a tiny mustard seed that a man planted in a garden; it grows and becomes a tree, and the birds make nests in its branches."

Jesus can make something great out of that little bit of faith you have!

AND that's a short one so here's another one for today...

Right now is the time for you to change the way you live. Here's Paul in Colossians.

Colossians 3:5-11
So put to death the sinful, earthly things lurking within you. Have nothing to do with sexual immorality, impurity, lust, and evil desires. Don't be greedy, for a greedy person is an idolater, worshiping the things of this world. Because of these sins, the anger of God is coming. You used to do these things when your life was still part of this world. But now is the time to get rid of anger, rage, malicious behavior, slander, and dirty language. Don't lie to each other, for you have stripped off your old sinful nature and all its wicked deeds. Put on your new nature, and be renewed as you learn to know your Creator and become like him. In this new life, it doesn't matter if you are a Jew or a Gentile, circumcised or uncircumcised, barbaric, uncivilized, slave, or free. Christ is all that matters, and he lives in all of us.

So take a second: What's one thing you can work on today? Christ lives in you.

Day 332

Ever feel like things are not going your way? Wondering if God is really listening to your prayers? Feel like you need someone to shine the light in your darkness? Don't worry. Help is on the way...

Psalm 121 (KJV)
I will lift up mine eyes unto the hills, from whence cometh my help.
My help cometh from the Lord, which made heaven and earth.
He will not suffer thy foot to be moved: he that keepeth thee will not slumber.
Behold, he that keepeth Israel shall neither slumber nor sleep.
The Lord is thy keeper: the Lord is thy shade upon thy right hand.
The sun shall not smite thee by day, nor the moon by night.
The Lord shall preserve thee from all evil: he shall preserve thy soul.
The Lord shall preserve thy going out and thy coming in from this time forth, and even for evermore.

God is always on the job. The maker of Heaven and Earth cares about YOU 24/7 to infinity and beyond. That's a promise you can count on.

Do you know for a fact that God is shining in your life? If so, take the time to pray a prayer of thanksgiving. If you are not certain, pick up your Bible and spend some more time listening to His Word.

Day 333

"Wisdom Here! Get your free wisdom." Don't you wish getting wisdom was that easy? Well, it just might be.

James 1:5-7
If you need wisdom, ask our generous God, and he will give it to you. He will not rebuke you for asking. But when you ask him, be sure that your faith is in God alone. Do not waver, for a person with divided loyalty is as unsettled as a wave of the sea that is blown and tossed by the wind. Such people should not expect to receive anything from the Lord.

Have you ever, as a child, asked your parents for advice to a question that you cleverly crafted to only produce one desired result but much to your dismay, your parents gave you quite another answer that you didn't really like? That's what it's like when we ask God for wisdom but don't really believe that His way is best, so we may or may not obey. If your faith is new or weak or struggling remember, you can trust God and his wisdom. Commit yourself to him with your whole heart and he will guide you.

Pray for wisdom today but be willing to accept what you are given, not what you necessarily want to be given.

Day 334

Revelation chapter 10 reveals that there is a Great Mystery. I'm a big fan of solving mysteries. It seems that to solve this one, you can't just pick and choose through verses in the Bible to suit your own needs.

Rev 10:7
…but in the days when the seventh angel is to blow his trumpet, The Mystery of God will be fulfilled, as he announced to his servants the prophets.

Has God been sending you subtle messages that He wants to have a stronger relationship with you? Studying the Bible will get you even closer to the Truth through His Word and this mystery will be revealed to YOU through HIM.

Take the time to sit with the Bible today and see what He reveals to you through His Word.

Day 335

So, you want to know how to get close to God? Well, read on.

James 4:7-8
Resist the devil, and he will flee from you. Come close to God, and God will come close to you. Wash your hands, you sinners; purify your hearts, for your loyalty is divided between God and the world.

Want to be closer? Well, come closer.

That's profound but chew on this too...

If the Love of Money is the Root of All Evil (1 Tim 6:10), what then can we define Riches by? Napoleon Hill does a good job of that in his book Think and Grow Rich. There he gives the top 12 definitions of Wealth and Riches according to him and I personally agree. I read this book when I was very young and have tried to live by it's advice. I would say it worked out very well. The number one definition of Wealth and Riches is a positive mental attitude. Mixed in there is the capacity for faith and the willingness to share one's blessings.

What are some of your definitions of Riches and Wealth?

Day 336

Hey, did you know that if you are a Christian, you've been adopted spiritually? Into God's family! He took you in, and made you His own. Paul talks about this in his letter to the church in Ephesus.

Ephesians 2:19-22
So now you Gentiles are no longer strangers and foreigners. You are citizens along with all of God's holy people. You are members of God's family. Together, we are his house, built on the foundation of the apostles and the prophets. And the cornerstone is Christ Jesus himself. We are carefully joined together in him, becoming a holy temple for the Lord. Through him you Gentiles are also being made part of this dwelling where God lives by his Spirit.

Adoption is a big deal! One couple I know is so excited about an adoption they are working on right now. Their hearts are full of love and excitement. It is a time of expectancy and they have found that it will not be an easy process but they are committed to the outcome. Being adopted into God's family is a big deal too. It's not always easy but it is definitely worthwhile.

We are part of the dwelling place of the Lord. What can we do to become a more perfect building block in the dwelling today?

Day 337

Mary, Mary, tell me how your garden grows... When you plant a garden, typically your carrot seeds will grow carrots, tomato seeds will grow tomatoes, and mustard will grow mustard, ketchup seeds will grow ketchup, and ...you get the idea.   God works in much the same way...

Galatians 6:7-10
Don't be misled--you cannot mock the justice of God. You will always harvest what you plant. Those who live only to satisfy their own sinful nature will harvest decay and death from that sinful nature. But those who live to please the Spirit will harvest everlasting life from the Spirit. So let's not get tired of doing what is good. At just the right time we will reap a harvest of blessing if we don't give up. Therefore, whenever we have the opportunity, we should do good to everyone--especially to those in the family of faith.

Be a diligent gardener! Be sure to plant the seeds that you want to harvest in the spring. For what you sow, you shall also surely reep.

What are you sowing today? Write down a few of your "seed" here:

Day 338

Today I want to share a little about how we read the Bible through a Big word...

Her·me·neu·tic Pronounced: hərmə'n(y)o͞odik/
noun
- a method or theory of interpretation.
Origin: Greek and Latin
late 17th century: from Greek hermēneutikos, from hermēneuein 'interpret.'

I consider myself a "Jesus Freak". In my one year in seminary school I learned that although we all read the same book (the Bible) we do so through rose colored glasses. These glasses we wear are called our Hermeneutic. My Hermeneutic is LOVE. When I read the Bible I do so looking at everything from the point of view of God's love for all his children. Some people's hermeneutic is Faith or Justice or Grace or Redeemed or Obedience... As a result, they may interpret the Bible and the world around us differently and some posts they make on Facebook may come off as offensive. (occasionally to me too).

I truly believe that in the end, that being the end of time or just the end of our time, we will see that God LOVES ALL of his children just as we love all our children and the people that made comments which may have offended us will be Grateful for the Grace they received through Faith instead of the Justice they Deserved for their dis-Obedience when they too are Redeemed.

What is your Hermeneutic? Give it some thought and write it down here:

Day 339

Have you ever had a secret you didn't want to keep in but you had to. One of those big, juicy ones that keeps threatening to sneak out? Well, the disciples experienced a situation a little like that.

Acts 4:18
So they called the apostles back in and commanded them never again to speak or teach in the name of Jesus.
Now, what Peter and John were telling people wasn't so much a secret; it was the Gospel. The problem was that the religious leaders of the day weren't super-happy about it. And so they tried to shut the apostles down. But that didn't work.

Acts 4:19-20
But Peter and John replied, "Do you think God wants us to obey you rather than him? We cannot stop telling about everything we have seen and heard."

We also live in a culture that wants us to stop talking about Jesus. So think about it.

Who are you going to obey?

What secrets are you keeping?

Day 340

If you're not sure you're doing what God's planned for you--and who hasn't
questioned that once or twice...

Psalm 127:1-2
Unless the LORD builds a house,
the work of the builders is wasted.
Unless the LORD protects a city,
guarding it with sentries will do no good.
It is useless for you to work so hard
from early morning until late at night,
anxiously working for food to eat;
for God gives rest to his loved ones.

If what you are doing is producing good things for the world, your
community or even a single individual, you are doing God's work. If you
were not doing God's work, it would not be producing fruit. If what you are
doing is not producing fruit, stay in prayer, with thanksgiving and your
work will be revealed to you in His time.

Is your work producing fruit?

Day 341

There is SO much to be stressed out about in this world. Think about what you might have been watching on TV 25 years ago compared to what is on TV today. That's just one example. Work, money, relationships... it can often seem too much to bear but...

1 Peter 5:6-7
So humble yourselves under the mighty power of God, and at the right time he will lift you up in honor. Give all your worries and cares to God, for he cares about you.

God loves you so much that He decided to bear the full weight of your worries, cares and sins. He already took them to the grave with Him and left them there as He rose and ascended into Heaven where He continues to love and care for you. And all God's grateful people said, "WOW"!!

What stressors do you need to surrender to God today? Take a minute to list them here:

Day 342

It's important to pray to God when things are going bad, but it's just as important to remember to praise him when things are good.

Here's an example from:
Psalm 30:1-5
I will exalt you, LORD, for you rescued me.
You refused to let my enemies triumph over me.
O LORD my God, I cried to you for help,
and you restored my health.
You brought me up from the grave, O LORD.
You kept me from falling into the pit of death.
Sing to the LORD, all you godly ones!
Praise his holy name.
For his anger lasts only a moment,
but his favor lasts a lifetime!
Weeping may last through the night,
but joy comes with the morning.

I think perhaps the hardest time to give praise and thanks is when things are not going our way. When things seem unfair and life is becoming harder than you think you can bear, that is indeed the hardest time to get on your knees and pray a sincere prayer of thanks but that is often the time when a prayer of thanksgiving helps the most.

Lord God, help us to see the big picture. Please remind us that you are in control and All Things will work out in the end for our good. Lord today we praise you, we glorify you, we worship your Holy Name. Thank you, Thank you, Thank you for all that you have done, all that you are doing and all that you will do. In Jesus' name, Amen.

Day 343

Hey, how does it make you feel when you do something for someone else and they don't even say Thank You? Paul reminds us to make thanksgiving a way of life.

Ephesians 5:20
And give thanks for everything to God the Father in the name of our Lord Jesus Christ.

He loves you. He provides for you. Let him know you're grateful.

PS- Thank you for reading my "one minute Bible studies" ☺ :)

Here's one more minute…

Tolerance…this is a tough one too. There are clearly verses in the Bible that demand we stand strong and not tolerate injustices. There are verses that call us to action and remind us that it is necessary to Judge those that are doing wrong, to correct them so that they can improve themselves. BUT…Jesus reminds us not to judge lest we be judged. What then shall we do?

Proverbs 17:15
He who justifies the wicked and he who condemns the righteous are both alike an abomination to the Lord.

John 8:7
And as they continued to ask him, he stood up and said to them, "Let him who is without sin among you be the first to throw a stone at her."

The world that we live in often seems to cry for tolerance. The Bible suggest we DO NOT tolerate the Sin. I believe that what looks like two different pieces of advice is really just one teaching from Jesus… HATE THE SIN BUT LOVE THE SINNER…

Day 344

He is the God who said:

Exodus 3:14
"I AM WHO I AM."

John 14:6
"I am the way, the truth, and the life. No one can come to the Father except through me."

Exodus 20:3
"You must not have any other god but me."

Psalm 46:10
"Be still, and know that I am God!
I will be honored by every nation.
I will be honored throughout the world."

So, this IS the one true God. He wants to be the only God in your life. That means "gods" such as money, pride, self, achievement or status. What's ruling your life right now?

It's something to think about today.

Day 345

You know how it is when you're watching politicians on TV pass the blame. All trying to make themselves look like they did everything right. We hate when politicians do that, but sometimes, we are right there with them.

1 John 1:7-10
But if we are living in the light, as God is in the light, then we have fellowship with each other, and the blood of Jesus, his Son, cleanses us from all sin.
If we claim we have no sin, we are only fooling ourselves and not living in the truth. But if we confess our sins to him, he is faithful and just to forgive us our sins and to cleanse us from all wickedness. If we claim we have not sinned, we are calling God a liar and showing that his word has no place in our hearts.

God wants to forgive you and me. So, live in the light. Confess and feel the peace of God's mercy.

What do you feel you need to confess today? Share it here in writing and ask God to forgive you of these things:

Day 346

Nebuchadnezzar was a foreign king who ruled some of the Jews in exile. God interacted with Nebuchadnezzar through Daniel the Jewish prophet. At a point where Nebuchadnezzar was getting too arrogant and forgetting God, he began to lose his mind. Daniel recorded this account of Nebuchadnezzar coming back to God:

Daniel 4:34-35
"After this time had passed, I, Nebuchadnezzar, looked up to heaven. My sanity returned, and I praised and worshiped the Most High and honored the one who lives forever.
His rule is everlasting,
and his kingdom is eternal.
All the people of the earth
are nothing compared to him.
He does as he pleases
among the angels of heaven
and among the people of the earth.
No one can stop him or say to him,
'What do you mean by doing these things?'"

God is all powerful. He will not be mocked. He can take even the most powerful, arrogant person and show his power through them. May we never give up hope and never lose faith in what God can do.

Know anyone that might be getting a little too full of themselves? I saw a guy in the mirror this morning that might have been going in that direction…

Day 347

Ever heard the word omnipotent? It means "having unlimited power" and it's usually a word that refers to God. But look who else fits the bill.

Matthew 28:18-20
Jesus came and told his disciples, "I have been given complete authority in heaven and on earth. Therefore, go and make disciples of all the nations, baptizing them in the name of the Father and the Son and the Holy Spirit. Teach these new disciples to obey all the commands I have given you. And be sure of this: I am with you always, even to the end of the age."

As powerful as he is, Jesus is with us, always, to help us do what he asks: the privilege of telling people about him.

Who have you told today?

Day 348

Crawling through the dark, you become aware of the power of even just a single solitary light. Something even as small as the flame from a lighter can be indispensable and light your path. John poetically opens his Gospel writing about light, life and the Word:

John 1:1-5
In the beginning the Word already existed.
The Word was with God,
and the Word was God.
He existed in the beginning with God.
God created everything through him,
and nothing was created except through him.
The Word gave life to everything that was created,
and his life brought light to everyone.
The light shines in the darkness,
and the darkness can never extinguish it.

Jesus was that light, that blinding light, that provided life, even as he was the Word that existed from before all. In him there is no darkness, and we walk, not crawl.

You are a bright light with Him in you. Go shine today!

Day 349

I can't imagine shepherds are the most sociable of folk. I mean, they spend most of their time with sheep. Not really the kind of occupation an extrovert chooses. But when some angels told a group of shepherds about the birth of Jesus, the experience was so transformative they couldn't help but tell everyone.

Luke 2:15-18
When the angels had returned to heaven, the shepherds said to each other, "Let's go to Bethlehem! Let's see this thing that has happened, which the Lord has told us about."

They hurried to the village and found Mary and Joseph. And there was the baby, lying in the manger. After seeing him, the shepherds told everyone what had happened and what the angel had said to them about this child. All who heard the shepherds' story were astonished.

You may not be a shepherd, and you probably weren't at the birth of Jesus, but it's a safe bet that he's done some transforming in your life. So tell someone about it. You might be surprised who listens.

Didn't you hear me? What are you still reading this for? Go tell someone!

Day 350

Abraham took his only son, Isaac to a special place, bound him up and trusted God so far as to raise a knife to sacrifice his son. God saw his willingness to obey sent an angel to tell Abraham to stop what he was doing. God also provided a ram, stuck in a thicket, for Abraham to sacrifice instead of his son.

Genesis 22:14
14 Abraham called the name of that place The Lord Will Provide, as it is said to this day, "In the mount of the Lord it will be provided."

So many deep concepts there. Obeying God, complete trust in God, willingness to sacrifice what is dear to us for God, being a true servant... But what I love most is "The Lord Will Provide"...Jehovah Jireh...Yahweh-yireh...יְהֹוָה יִרְאֶה... Before, now and forever The Lord Will Provide for all our needs.

God is good...All the time!

And the response:

And All the time...God is Good!

What would you be willing to sacrifice for God if asked to do so?

Day 351

Of all things we have to worry about, money is one of the most common. I read somewhere that finances are the reason for most couples breaking up. Bummer! While you're trying to be wise with your finances, don't forget this.

Hebrews 13:5
Don't love money; be satisfied with what you have. For God has said, "I will never fail you. I will never abandon you."

Put your trust completely in God. You will come to find that it is God alone that can satisfy your deepest hunger and quench your worst thirst. Money pales in comparison. As the Beetles sang… Money Can't Buy You Love…No, No, No, No! Say you don't need no diamond rings and God will be satisfied…well, not really…but you get the idea.

Who do you put your trust in?

Day 352

We live in a stressful world today. It seems that we are never at peace either within ourselves or within the world. Imagine if we could just live in body and a world that was completely at Peace...

John 16:33 ESV
I have said these things to you, that in me you may have peace. In the world you will have tribulation. But take heart; I have overcome the world."

And now may the Lord of peace himself give you peace at all times in every way. The Lord be with you all. (I think that's Biblical ☺)

What would peace look like in your life? There's plenty of room here to fully describe what a peaceful life would look like. Be as detailed as possible. Write your description down here:

Day 353

Ever Feel guilty about taking time to rest or to go on vacation? My wife and I are taking time to be alone with each other and to be alone with God this week. Are you taking time to Rest?

Matthew 11:29
Take my yoke upon you, and learn from me, for I am gentle and lowly in heart, and you will find rest for your souls.

Psalm 127:2
It is in vain that you rise up early and go late to rest, eating the bread of anxious toil; for he gives to his beloved sleep.

Mark 6:31
And he said to them, "Come away by yourselves to a desolate place and rest a while." For many were coming and going, and they had no leisure even to eat.

Exodus 34:21
"Six days you shall work, but on the seventh day you shall rest. In plowing time and in harvest you shall rest.

All work and no play makes Jack a dull boy...and God doesn't think its such a hot idea either.

Where have you been...Lately?

Day 354

Today I was meditating and praying on Tolerance. Ever had someone who really got on your "last nerve"? Ever found yourself gritting your teeth through a fake smile? If you had a chance and no one was looking, you would consider picking up a big rock and tossing it their way...

John 8:7
And as they continued to ask him, he stood up and said to them, "Let him who is without sin among you be the first to throw a stone at her."

Before you consider throwing a stone, take a good look introspectively. You know, those that live in Glass Houses shouldn't throw stones. Only one person in all of history is without sin and it sure ain't us!

Who do you think you could be a little more tolerant of in your life? Write it down here to give you more leverage to follow through.

Day 355

You know, one of the most frustrating things you can do is build a sandcastle. At first, you're like, "Woo-hoo! Sandcastles!" And then you get going and get the castle to be two stories high, or so. Then guess what? In comes the tide and your hard work crumbles before your weeping eyes. And you're stuck with a pile of wet sand wondering why anyone would ever try to build a house on sand. Jesus wondered the same thing.

Luke 6:47-49
"I will show you what it's like when someone comes to me, listens to my teaching, and then follows it. It is like a person building a house who digs deep and lays the foundation on solid rock. When the floodwaters rise and break against that house, it stands firm because it is well built. But anyone who hears and doesn't obey is like a person who builds a house without a foundation. When the floods sweep down against that house, it will collapse into a heap of ruins.'

Let's review: Sandcastles? Bad idea. Hearing Jesus but not obeying him? Yeah, not so good either.

What are some of the sandcastles in your life?

Day 356

So, I can get a little hot headed once in a while. When people say things about me or people I care about that are not true, it sends my blood pressure through the roof. My instinct is to judge the person telling the lies and condemn them. Can you relate?

James 4:11-12
Do not speak evil against one another, brothers. The one who speaks against a brother or judges his brother, speaks evil against the law and judges the law. But if you judge the law, you are not a doer of the law but a judge. There is only one lawgiver and judge, he who is able to save and to destroy. But who are you to judge your neighbor?

I have learned to take a deep breath and try to see it from the other person's perspective. Often it winds up better to just let it go. I repeat to myself, "Judge not lest ye be judged."

A little too judgmental? What can we do to leave the judgment to the one true judge?

Day 357

My office utilizes many payment options but the one that makes the most sense to me is the Box on the Wall, known as the GPC system. GPC stands for God-Patient-Chiropractic fee system where the patient decides what weekly payment they can afford and places that in the box each week before they are adjusted. My family never wanted for anything while we had the box on the wall and God always blessed us with all the manna we needed...

Deuteronomy 8:17-18
"He did all this so you would never say to yourself, 'I have achieved this wealth with my own strength and energy.' Remember the LORD your God. He is the one who gives you power to be successful, in order to fulfill the covenant he confirmed to your ancestors with an oath."

God owns my office, I am the servant. I'm here to testify that there is incredible FREEDOM in being the servant. Lets face it, we are all servants.

Who are you serving?

Day 358

At the very beginning of the Bible God stresses the importance of "being a blessing" as he speaks to Abraham in the 12th chapter of Genesis.
Sometimes all we need to do is plant a kind word to be a blessing and fulfill Jesus' great commission...

Matthew 28:19-20
19 Go ye therefore, and teach all nations, baptizing them in the name of the Father, and of the Son, and of the Holy Ghost: 20 Teaching them to observe all things whatsoever I have commanded you: and, lo, I am with you always, even unto the end of the world. Amen.

Yesterday my friend Andy told me that he had just been baptized and my Biblical posts had some small part in that. He could not have known how overwhelmed with JOY I was! Through his words, he was a blessing to me. It was as if I heard my Lord God and Savior, Jesus Christ encouraging me that my small ministry is helping to fulfill the great commission. More importantly, I am so very grateful that I know I will be able to worship with this great friend for eternity. Andy, God Bless you on this new journey as you walk with Christ.

You may never know how important your faith, words or actions are in the salvation of another person's soul.

Keep that in mind as you go through your day today.

Day 359

My wife and I have a fun way of kidding each other. I love the summer and she loves the winter. In November I tell her, "It's almost April". In April, she tells me, "Its almost November". We both long for the season we enjoy the most. But....

Ecclesiastes 7:10
Don't long for "the good old days."
This is not wise.

I once heard that those that live in the past, live with regret. Those that live in the future live with fear, but those that live in the PRESENT live in PEACE. Don't long for the good old days, don't worry about the future, live in the present...live in peace.

Are you looking back? Remember what happened to Lot's wife?

Day 360

Often times, well meaning friends or that little voice in your head will tempt you to do something that doesn't sit right in your gut. You know what the responsible thing to do is but in your weakened human state you find it hard to resist. Jesus fasted for 40 days, was tired and hungry when he was tempted...

Matthew 4:1-11:
Then Jesus was led up by the Spirit into the wilderness to be tempted by the devil. And he fasted forty days and forty nights, and afterward he was hungry. And the tempter came and said to him, "If you are the Son of God, command these stones to become loaves of bread." But he answered, "It is written, 'Man shall not live by bread alone, but by every word that proceeds from the mouth of God.'" Then the devil took him to the holy city, and set him on the pinnacle of the temple, and said to him, "If you are the Son of God, throw yourself down; for it is written:
'He will give his angels charge of you, and
On their hands they will bear you up,
lest you strike your foot against a stone.'"
Jesus said to him, "Again it is written, 'You shall not tempt the Lord your God.'" Again, the devil took him to a very high mountain, and showed him all the kingdoms of the world and the glory of them; and he said to him, "All these I will give you, if you will fall down and worship me." Then Jesus said to him, "Begone, Satan! for it is written, 'You shall worship the Lord your God and him only shall you serve.'" Then the devil left him, and behold, angels came and ministered to him.

Jesus' expression of trust and dependence on God is what makes human life make sense. God makes us human, Christ makes us Christians. When you put Christ back into a Christian, you put God back into the human. You are only human but with Christ, you can make better choices in your life.

Day 361

These words from Jesus really get to the heart of what giving is all about.

Matthew 6:1-4
"Watch out! Don't do your good deeds publicly, to be admired by others, for you will lose the reward from your Father in heaven. When you give to someone in need, don't do as the hypocrites do--blowing trumpets in the synagogues and streets to call attention to their acts of charity! I tell you the truth, they have received all the reward they will ever get. But when you give to someone in need, don't let your left hand know what your right hand is doing. Give your gifts in private, and your Father, who sees everything, will reward you."

When you give publicly, people say, "thank you." When you give secretly, people say, "thank God."

What will you give secretly today?

AND a bonus for today…

I have found that people are looking for "Peace and Happiness" in their lives. I also know that the more we give something away, the more we will receive. Maybe we should pray this ancient prayer for more people we care about...

Numbers 6:24 – 27 The Lord bless you and keep you; the Lord make his face to shine upon you, and be gracious to you; the Lord lift up his countenance upon you, and give you peace.

The giving hand is never empty... I pray you have peace and happiness fill your life abundantly.

Day 362

I was meditating on Communion tonight. What do we really experience when we break a little piece of bread (more like Styrofoam these days) and take a sip of grape juice? Sometimes we do it because it is the "thing to do" and it is done mindlessly as something we have done, and will do by rote instead of how Jesus intended...

1 Corinthians 11:23-26
For I pass on to you what I received from the Lord himself. On the night when he was betrayed, the Lord Jesus took some bread and gave thanks to God for it. Then he broke it in pieces and said, "This is my body, which is given for you. Do this to remember me." In the same way, he took the cup of wine after supper, saying, "This cup is the new covenant between God and his people--an agreement confirmed with my blood. Do this to remember me as often as you drink it." For every time you eat this bread and drink this cup, you are announcing the Lord's death until he comes again.

Wow...that is intense! It symbolizes the blood that was shed for our sins and a body that was broken to save someone that did not deserve such a sacrifice. It was done for me and for you. Before you take communion next time, really consider the sacrifice that was made on your behalf. Make it personal...God so loved you that He gave his only Son. His Son...think about that before breaking the bread or drinking of the cup. God loves more deeply than you can ever understand.

Day 363

My prayer for my children has always been that they find the "reason they were put on Earth by God". That they find their Purpose. I pray that for you too...

Romans 12:6-8
Having gifts that differ according to the grace given to us, let us use them: if prophecy, in proportion to our faith; if service, in our serving; the one who teaches, in his teaching; the one who exhorts, in his exhortation; the one who contributes, in generosity; the one who leads, with zeal; the one who does acts of mercy, with cheerfulness.

Our purpose in life, as God originally created man, is 1) glorify God and enjoy fellowship with Him, 2) have good relationships with others, 3) work, and 4) have dominion over the earth. But with man's fall into sin, fellowship with God is broken, relationships with others are strained, work seems to always be frustrating, and man struggles to maintain any semblance of dominion over nature. It was only by restoring my fellowship with God, through faith in Jesus Christ, that my purpose in life was rediscovered. I hope that helps someone today.

What is your purpose in life?

Day 364

Recently I was upset by doctors hiding behind their contracts and covenants with "health insurance companies" to rationalize accepting less money from the insurance company than they accept from a cash paying patient for the same service. This is what the Bible has to say about that..

Numbers 30:2
"If a man vow a vow unto the LORD, or swear an oath to bind his soul with a bond; he shall not break his word, he shall do according to all that proceedeth out of his mouth."

Romans 13:8
Owe no man any thing, but Love one another: for he that loves one another has fulfilled the law

The Hippocratic Oath, or some form of it, is uttered by all that get a health degree but how many really keep that oath? All of us have signed contracts as a "necessary evil" (mortgages, credit cards, provider agreements...) but how many of us have upheld our contract with God to Love one another unconditionally?

Have we entered into any contracts that we are not proud of?

Day 365

We all have a "cross to bear." In today's day in age, we all carry heavy burdens, we have all endured hard times and criticism. There are, however, few among us that would have laid their life down to obediently and willingly save others if we knew we had the ability to summon all the power of Heaven and Earth to protect us from having to endure the pain and suffering.

Hebrews 12:2
Looking unto Jesus the author and finisher of our faith; who for the joy that was set before him endured the cross, despising the shame, and is set down at the right hand of the throne of God.

There are few among the many. Are you among the few? If you have not made a decision to be "All In" with Christ, consider what He endured for you so that you could put down your cross, be forgiven of the things you regret having done, and have eternal life in union with Him. If you are ready to let Jesus into your heart today, go here--
> http://www.allaboutgod.com/prayer-of-salvation.htm and become among the few.

A Few More...

The chiropractic lasting Purpose is to give for the sake of giving, Love for the sake of loving, serve for the sake of serving without any expectation of compensation so that others can live their life more abundantly.

Luke 6:38
Give, and it will be given to you. They will pour into your lap a good measure—pressed down, shaken together, and running over. For by your standard of measure it will be measured to you in return."

John 3:16
"For God so loved the world, that He gave His only begotten Son, that whoever believes in Him shall not perish, but have eternal life.

1 Peter 4:10
As each one has received a special gift, employ it in serving one another as good stewards of the manifold grace of God.

Give- Love- Serve out of your abundance...

Do you have a dream you never pursued? Something that seemed so unattainable that you just gave up on it? Is there greatness inside of you still waiting to express itself? What would you do if you knew you could not fail?

Romans 12:6-8
We have different gifts, according to the grace given to each of us. If your gift is prophesying, then prophesy in accordance with your faith; if it is serving, then serve; if it is teaching, then teach; if it is to encourage, then give encouragement; if it is giving, then give generously; if it is to lead, do it diligently; if it is to show mercy, do it cheerfully.

God has placed a dream in your heart and talent in your mind, if you pursue your dream as a humble and obedient servant, nothing is impossible. Your only job now is to rediscover your dream.

This One From Father Mathew Glover I Simply Could Not Leave Out…

This morning, Father <u>Matthew Glover</u> gave a sermon that really touched many hearts. It was one of those sermons that you wish you could have recorded and watched over and over again. At the end of the mass, everyone actually applauded (I haven't seen that in a long while even though God deserves more than just a round of applause).

He touched so many subjects including Love and Fear but what spoke to me most was the subject of being PRESENT. Today we are distracted by so many things. Technology (even the time you spend reading this message) takes us away from the relationships we care about most. We spend time texting, e-mailing, posting on Facebook, twitter and all the other online media and it takes us away from being present, truly nurturing the relationships in our lives.

God loved us so much that He came to be with us through His Son. He came to be FULLY PRESENT with us. Not by texting us, not by messaging us, not by e-mailing us, but by being truly here, in the flesh, fully present with us. He loved us so much that He fully experienced life and death with and for us. It is so important to remember that He is still here, FULLY PRESENT with us. By that example He is calling to YOU and to ME to be FULLY PRESENT with Him, un-distracted by all this technology. He is also calling to you and to me to be fully present in our relationships with our spouse, our children, our parents, our family, our friends and those of his children who are without friends and family.

Father Matt called us to give the gift that Our Lord God Himself gave to us. A gift that is costly. It will cost the one thing we value most, more than money or things...our TIME. This Christ-mas, give those you love most dearly, your complete, un-distracted, un-divided, focused TIME as you are FULLY PRESENT with them. (YES, that means you have to turn off the computer now and go be present with those you care about including God.)

Thank you Father Matt. May God continue to Bless your Ministry Richly and I hope we dedicate TIME to break bread and be fully present with God together this year.

One more...

Another great sermon at Church this morning. We lit the first Advent candle which Father Matt reminded us was to admonish us to begin preparing for the birth of our Savior. He also reminded us not to wait for candles to be lit before we start praying...

Mark 13:33-37 (NKJV)
Take heed, watch and pray; for you do not know when the time is. It is like a man going to a far country, who left his house and gave authority to his servants, and to each his work, and commanded the doorkeeper to watch. Watch therefore, for you do not know when the master of the house is coming—in the evening, at midnight, at the crowing of the rooster, or in the morning— lest, coming suddenly, he find you sleeping. And what I say to you, I say to all: Watch!"

Even before Jesus' birth, God knew how his life would play out here on Earth. What type of love did that take? Now it's your turn and all you have to do is take heed, watch and pray. Don't let your faith fall asleep. Haven't prayed lately...take a moment and do it now.

Stopped going to church?
... make plans not to make any plans next Sunday and I will see you there.

OK, Just One More...

Sometimes we feel so much to be thankful for and our hearts are so full that it is difficult to put into words how we feel. The psalmist suggests in Psalm 100 offering God this prayer:

Psalm 100:1-5 A Psalm for giving thanks.
Make a joyful noise to the Lord, all the earth! Serve the Lord with gladness! Come into his presence with singing! Know that the Lord, he is God! It is he who made us, and we are his; we are his people, and the sheep of his pasture. Enter his gates with thanksgiving, and his courts with praise! Give thanks to him; bless his name! For the Lord is good; his steadfast love endures forever, and his faithfulness to all generations.

Not all of us are going to feel as though we are in a season of our lives where we can easily give thanks but we as a people, as children of the most high God, are called to give thanks ALWAYS. We are called to give thanks in both the good and the bad times with a deep faith and a knowing that God is Good All the time. Pray a prayer of Thanksgiving today and share with God the substance of the things you hope for eagerly awaiting the evidence of things not yet seen.

Happy Thanksgiving to all my friends and family. In Health and Faith, Jay

May every day be a day to give thanks throughout the year.

A Revelation From Revelation I Felt Compelled To Add. It Was A Game Changer For Me...

This is a long one but a true revelation for me...

I have been doing a Men's Bible study of Revelation with Wheeler V. and Paul B. here in Rhode Island. I wanted to let everyone know that they are welcome if they are in the Warwick, RI area on Thursday morning at 8 AM. We meet at Chick-fil-A and it is an all or none thing. If one of us has to miss, we cancel that week so check the night before with one of us.

Two weeks ago I had an epiphany of sorts during the study. It made all the years of study and ALL the Bible verses that were once difficult...easy to understand. In Revelation Chapter 10 we began talking about what the 7 thunders might have said and what the mystery of God might be. Somehow we stumbled upon the idea that the mystery and information in the thunder is the understanding that the new creation after Revelation is not like anything we can perceive here in this time and in this world. The new creation is a whole different thing. It is not an organization composed of people it is a new Organism. It is a single body with Jesus as the head. We will be like the cells that make up that pure, perfect body.

That makes so many other passages make sense to me. In the Old Testament, I was appalled at the very idea that God would wipe out tens of thousands of people, his children, in a single blow. I was appalled at Him killing all living things except for Noah and his family in the great flood. BUT, when you see it from the point of ultimately wanting to form one, perfect, sinless body...one perfect, sinless organism AND the fact that God is perfect justice at the same time He is perfect grace, it all makes sense. God loved those people, his children, and I'm sure it pained Him to have to wipe them out but it had to be done. It is like someone having prostate cancer... You love all the cells in your body including the prostate but if the prostate is cancer ridden and you leave it in the body, it will kill the rest of the body. You hope and pray for a miracle but if the cells don't heal and become healthy, you must, no matter how much it upsets you, have the prostate removed or it will kill all the rest of the cells including the head and you will die.

Time and time again, God tells his people to follow His command. They do not and continue to sin so he must wipe them out so that they do not corrupt the people that have followed His command. Over and over this plays out in the Old Testament until God finally realized that any creation with free will is subject to and will fall prey to sin. In one GREAT, PAINFUL,

SELFLESS act, He sends His Son, as the sacrificial Lamb so that He can maintain perfect justice and still offer perfect grace through Jesus for those that choose to accept it. In this one act, He affords those that sin a chance to repent and believe in his Son so that they can be washed clean of their sins and still be part of the Organism, the new creation to come.

Other passages become clear with this concept of Organism vs. Organization like when Jesus is asked in Luke 20, "Teacher, Moses wrote for us that if a man's brother dies, having a wife but no children, the man must take the widow and raise up offspring for his brother. 29 Now there were seven brothers. The first took a wife, and died without children. 30 And the second 31 and the third took her, and likewise all seven left no children and died. 32 Afterward the woman also died. 33 In the resurrection, therefore, whose wife will the woman be? For the seven had her as wife." Essentially Jesus says that they totally don't get it. It's not like that after the resurrection. It's not about husbands and wives; it is a new creation, a new organism where we are all part of the perfect body with Him as the head.

Think for yourself of a tough verse in the Bible. Apply the goal of having one perfect, sinless body and what God would have to do to remain perfectly just in that situation and all becomes much easier (to me).

I, for one, am looking forward to being part of the body in the new creation. Revelation is a great book to study. Once I thought it was just the ramblings of a man on a bad drug induced trip. Now, on closer investigation, it appears to be the book that makes sense of all the rest. As much as it reveals, it still keeps for us grand secrets that will be brought to light for us at the right time and in the right place.

Holy, Holy, Holy! The Lord God is Holy. WOW! For we know in part, and we prophesy in part. But when that which is perfect is come, then that which is in part shall be done away. -1Cor 13:9-10
In Health and Faith, Jay

Notes:

Notes:

Notes:

Notes:

Made in the USA
Middletown, DE
06 October 2017